ITALIAN COOKING

ITALIAN COOKING

MORE THAN 70 DELICIOUSLY AUTHENTIC RECIPES FROM ALL OVER ITALY SHOWN STEP BY STEP IN OVER 300 PHOTOGRAPHS

JENI WRIGHT AND ANGELA BOGGIANO

HERMES HOUSE

This edition is published by Hermes House, an imprint of Anness Publishing Ltd,
Hermes House, 88–89 Blackfriars Road, London SE1 8HA
tel. 020 7401 2077; fax 020 7633 9499
www.hermeshouse.com; www.annesspublishing.com

Publisher: Joanna Lorenz
Editors: Elizabeth Woodland and Dan Hurst
Designer: Siân Keogh
Photographers: William Lingwood and Janine Hosegood
Home Economist: Lucy McKelvie, assisted by Sophie Wheeler
Stylist: Marian Price
Production Controller: Mai-Ling Collyer

Main front cover main image shows Tagliatelle with Bolognese Sauce
– for recipe see page 158

Previously published as part of a larger volume, *The Italian Kitchen Bible*

Notes

For all recipes, quantities are given in both metric and imperial measures and, where appropriate, in standard cups and spoons. Follow one set of measures, but not a mixture, because they are not interchangeable.

Standard spoon and cup measures are level.

1 tsp = 5ml, 1 tbsp = 15ml, 1 cup = 250ml/8fl oz.

Australian standard tablespoons are 20ml. Australian readers should use 3 tsp in place of 1 tbsp for measuring small quantities.

American pints are 16fl oz/2 cups. American readers should use 20fl oz/2.5 cups in place of 1 pint when measuring liquids.

Electric oven temperatures in this book are for conventional ovens. When using a fan oven, the temperature will probably need to be reduced by about 10–20°C/20–40°F. Since ovens vary, you should check with your manufacturer's instruction book for guidance.

Medium (US large) eggs are used unless otherwise stated.(The recipe for Tiramisu on page 86 contains raw eggs and should be avoided by pregnant women, children and anyone who is unwell).

Contents

Introduction

Italian cookery reflects the fact that the country was unified only in 1861. Until then, each region produced its own characteristic cuisine, relying exclusively on ingredients that could be gathered, cultivated or reared locally. Nowadays, of course, regional produce can be easily transported all over the country, but Italians still prefer to base their cooking on local ingredients, because they regard quality and freshness as more important than diversity and innovation. So the most flavoursome sun-ripened tomatoes, aubergines and peppers are still found in the south, the freshest seafood is on offer along the coast, the finest hams come from the area where the pigs are raised, and so on.

La cucina italiana remains distinctly regional; northern Italian cooking, for example, incorporates ingredients that are simply never found in the recipes of Sicily and Naples, and vice-versa. In the dairy-farming north, butter is used in place of the olive oil so prevalent in the south; bread and polenta are eaten instead of pasta. The unifying feature is the insistence on high quality ingredients. Good food has always been essential to the Italian way of life. *La cucina italiana* is one of the oldest cooking cultures in the world, dating back to the ancient Greeks and perhaps even earlier.

This Italian butcher's shop (below) not only sells the local *cinghiale* (wild boar), but also cured meats, cheeses and other essential cooking ingredients.

The Romans adored food and often ate and drank to excess; it was they who really laid the foundations of Italian and European cuisine. The early Romans were peasant farmers who ate only the simple, rustic foods they could produce, like grain, cheeses and olives. For them, meat was an unheard-of luxury; animals were bred to work in the fields and were too precious to eat. Trading links with other parts of the world, however, encouraged Roman farmers to cultivate new vegetables and fruits and, of course, vines, while their trade in salt and exotic spices enabled them to preserve and pickle all kinds of meat, game and fish. Food became a near-obsession and ever more elaborate dishes were devised to be served at the decadent and orgiastic banquets for which the Romans were famed. The decline and fall of the Roman Empire led inevitably to a deterioration in the quality of cooking and a return to simple, basic foods. For centuries, regional cuisine reverted to its original uncomplicated style.

With the Renaissance came great wealth and a new interest in elaborate food. Once again, rich families strove to outdo each other with lavish banquets where courses of rich, extravagant foods were served - truffles, song-birds, game, desserts dripping with honey and spices - all washed down with quantities of wine. The poor, of course, continued to subsist

Olives (top) growing in groves along-side grape vines on an Umbrian hillside, and a selection of cured sausages and air-dried *prosciutto* hanging in store (above) are just two of the vast array of traditional Italian ingredients that are now exported around the world.

Italian cooks insist on high-quality cooking ingredients and even local delicatessens (right) are packed full of fresh and preserved ingredients and other foods – fruity cakes and crisp biscuits, such as *panforte* and *cantucci*, dried *fagioli* (beans), flavourful olive oils and vinegars, *prosciutto crudo* (cured hams), traditional cheeses, such as *Parmigiano Reggiano*, pickles and preserves, marinated olives, canned tomatoes and bottled sauces.

The sun-drenched southern regions of Italy provide essential store cupboard ingredients, such as full-flavoured green and black olives and delicious sun-dried tomatoes.

on the simple foods they had always eaten, but the wealthier middle classes developed a taste for fine foods and created their own bourgeois dishes. The finer features of Italian cooking even reached the French, when Catherine de' Medici went to Paris to marry the future Henri II, taking fifty of her own cooks with her. They introduced new ingredients and cooking techniques to France and in return learnt the art of French cuisine. In those regions of Italy which border France, you can still find reciprocal influences of French classical cooking, but, generally speaking, Italians do not like elaborately sauced dishes, preferring to let the natural flavours of their raw ingredients speak for themselves.

The essence of Italian cooking today is simplicity. The Italian way of cooking fish is a good example of this. In coastal areas, freshly caught fish is most often simply chargrilled over hot coals, then served with nothing more than a splash of extra virgin olive oil, a wedge of lemon and freshly ground black pepper. Recipes like *branzino al forno*, in which the fish is so delicious that any elaborate sauce would mask its delicate flavour, and *gamberi fritti in padella*, where the robust texture of sweet and juicy prawns (shrimp) are partnered with a simple tomato sauce to compliment rather than obscure the fresh taste of the fish, are typically simple.

Italians learn to appreciate good food when they are young children, and eating is one of the major pleasures of the day, no matter what the day of the week or time of the year. Witness an Italian family gathered around the Sunday lunch table in a local restaurant, and consider how the Italian menu of *antipasto* followed by pasta, rice or gnocchi, then fish, meat and vegetables served in sequence is devised so that each can be savoured separately – both the food and the occasion are to be enjoyed as long as possible. The first course, or *antipasto*, is a unique feature. In restaurants, this can be a vast array of different dishes, both hot and cold, from which diners can choose as few or as many as they wish. At home with the family, it is more likely to be a slice or two of *salami* or *prosciutto crudo* with fresh figs or melon if these are in season. But no matter how humble or grand the setting or the occasion, the *antipasto* is always visually tempting. Dishes like *verdura marinata per antipasto* and *peperoni arrostiti con pesto*, which look so attractive, are typical in this way.

The variety and diversity of the Italian ingredients available in supermarkets and delicatessens will surely inspire you to concoct any number of delicious meals, from a simple dish of pasta to a four-course dinner. A plate of *antipasto* followed by pasta or risotto flavoured with seasonal ingredients, then simply-cooked meat or fish and finally a local cheese and fruit, make a veritable feast. You could prepare a different meal along these lines every day of the year and almost never repeat the same combination. You don't need to visit Italy to prepare a menu full of the flavours of the country, the delicious recipes on the following pages will allow you to experiment with the delights of regional Italian cooking from your own kitchen.

FRESH INGREDIENTS ARE HIGHLY PRIZED BY ITALIAN COOKS AND ARE OFTEN SOLD FROM THE LOCAL OUTDOOR MARKETS: DOZENS OF *CARCIOFI* (GLOBE ARTICHOKES) ARE TIED READY FOR TRANSPORT TO A LOCAL MARKET (BELOW), AND AN OUTDOOR STALL IS PILED HIGH WITH A TYPICALLY WIDE SELECTION OF HIGH-QUALITY FRESH HERBS AND SALAD LEAVES, VEGETABLES AND FRUITS (BOTTOM).

Soups and Antipasti

Soups and antipasti are integral to Italian cuisine. Hot or cold antipasti make perfect party food, and along with clear broth, brodo, and delicate puréed soups are the perfect start to any meal. More substantial chunky soups, *minestre*, are often main courses in themselves.

Onion Soup

La cipollata

This warming winter soup comes from Umbria, where it is sometimes thickened with beaten eggs and lots of grated Parmesan cheese. It is then served on top of hot toasted croûtes – rather like savoury scrambled eggs.

Ingredients

115 g/4 oz pancetta rashers, any rinds removed, roughly chopped
30 ml/2 tbsp olive oil
15 g/½ oz/1 tbsp butter
675 g/1½ lb onions, thinly sliced
10 ml/2 tsp sugar
about 1.2 litres/2 pints/5 cups chicken stock
350 g/12 oz ripe Italian plum tomatoes, peeled and roughly chopped
a few basil leaves, shredded
salt and freshly ground black pepper
freshly grated Parmesan cheese, to serve

serves 4

1 ▲ Put the chopped pancetta in a large saucepan and heat gently, stirring constantly, until the fat runs. Increase the heat to medium, add the oil, butter, onions and sugar and stir well to mix.

2 ▲ Half cover the pan and cook the onions gently for about 20 minutes until golden. Stir frequently and lower the heat if necessary.

3 ▲ Add the stock, tomatoes and salt and pepper and bring to the boil, stirring. Lower the heat, half cover the pan and simmer, stirring occasionally, for about 30 minutes.

4 Check the consistency of the soup and add a little more stock or water if it is too thick.

5 Just before serving, stir in most of the basil and taste for seasoning. Serve hot, garnished with the remaining shredded basil. Hand round the freshly grated Parmesan separately.

Cook's Tip

Look for Vidalia onions to make this soup. They are available at large supermarkets, and have a very sweet flavour and attractive yellowish flesh.

Cream of Courgette Soup

Vellutata di zucchini

The beauty of this soup is its delicate colour, rich and creamy texture and subtle taste. If you prefer a more pronounced cheese flavour, use Gorgonzola instead of Dolcelatte.

Ingredients
30 ml/2 tbsp olive oil
15 g/½ oz/1 tbsp butter
1 medium onion, roughly chopped
900 g/2 lb courgettes (zucchini), trimmed and sliced
5 ml/1 tsp dried oregano
600 ml/1 pint/2½ cups vegetable or chicken stock
115 g/4 oz Dolcelatte cheese, rind removed, diced
300 ml/½ pint/1¼ cups single (light) cream
salt and freshly ground black pepper
fresh oregano and extra Dolcelatte, to garnish
serves 4–6

1 ▲ Heat the oil and butter in a large saucepan until foaming. Add the onion and cook gently for about 5 minutes, stirring frequently, until softened but not brown.

2 ▲ Add the courgettes and oregano, with salt and pepper to taste. Cook over a medium heat for 10 minutes, stirring frequently.

3 ▲ Pour in the stock and bring to the boil, stirring. Lower the heat, half cover the pan and simmer gently, stirring occasionally, for about 30 minutes. Stir in the diced Dolcelatte until melted.

Cook's Tip
To save time, trim off and discard the ends of the courgettes, cut them into thirds, then chop in a food processor fitted with the metal blade.

4 ▲ Process the soup in a blender or food processor until smooth, then press through a sieve into a clean pan.

5 Add two-thirds of the cream and stir over a low heat until hot, but not boiling. Check the consistency and add more stock if the soup is too thick. Taste for seasoning, then pour into heated bowls. Swirl in the remaining cream. Garnish with oregano and extra cheese and serve.

Wild Mushroom Soup

Zuppa di porcini

Wild mushrooms are expensive; you could use some cultivated ones, if you like, but keep the dried porcini for their intense flavour. The beef stock may seem unusual in a vegetable soup, but it helps to strengthen the earthy flavour of the mushrooms.

Ingredients

25 g/1 oz/2 cups dried porcini mushrooms
30 ml/2 tbsp olive oil
15 g/½ oz/1 tbsp butter
2 leeks, thinly sliced
2 shallots, roughly chopped
1 garlic clove, roughly chopped
225 g/8 oz/3 cups fresh wild mushrooms
about 1.2 litres/2 pints/5 cups beef stock
2.5 ml/½ tsp dried thyme
150 ml/¼ pint/⅔ cup double (heavy) cream
salt and freshly ground black pepper
fresh thyme sprigs, to garnish
serves 4

Cook's Tip

Porcini are ceps. Italian cooks would make this soup with a combination of fresh and dried ceps, but if fresh ceps are difficult to obtain, you can use other wild mushrooms, such as chanterelles.

1 ▲ Put the dried porcini in a bowl, add 250 ml/8 fl oz/1 cup warm water and leave to soak for 20 - 30 minutes. Lift out of the liquid and squeeze over the bowl to remove as much of the soaking liquid as possible. Strain all the liquid and reserve to use later. Finely chop the porcini.

2 Heat the oil and butter in a large saucepan until foaming. Add the sliced leeks, chopped shallots and garlic and cook gently for about 5 minutes, stirring frequently, until softened but not coloured.

3 ▲ Chop or slice the fresh mushrooms and add to the pan. Stir over a medium heat for a few minutes until they begin to soften. Pour in the stock and bring to the boil. Add the porcini, soaking liquid, dried thyme and salt and pepper. Lower the heat, half cover the pan and simmer gently for 30 minutes, stirring occasionally.

4 ▲ Pour about three-quarters of the soup into a blender or food processor and process until smooth. Return to the soup remaining in the pan, slowly stir in the cream and heat through. Check the consistency and add more stock if the soup is too thick. Taste for seasoning. Serve hot, garnished with thyme sprigs.

Tomato and Fresh Basil Soup

Crema di pomodori al basilico

A soup for late summer when fresh tomatoes are at their most flavoursome.

Ingredients

15 ml/1 tbsp olive oil
25 g/1 oz/2 tbsp butter
1 medium onion, finely chopped
900 g/2 lb ripe Italian plum tomatoes, roughly chopped
1 garlic clove, roughly chopped
about 750 ml/1¼ pints/3 cups chicken or vegetable stock
120 ml/4 fl oz/½ cup dry white wine
30 ml/2 tbsp sun-dried tomato paste
30 ml/2 tbsp shredded fresh basil, plus a few whole leaves, to garnish
150 ml/¼ pint/⅔ cup double (heavy) cream
salt and freshly ground black pepper

serves 4–6

1 ▲ Heat the oil and butter in a large saucepan until foaming. Add the onion and cook gently for about 5 minutes, stirring frequently, until softened but not brown.

2 ▲ Stir in the chopped tomatoes and garlic, then add the stock, white wine and sun-dried tomato paste, with salt and pepper to taste. Bring to the boil, then lower the heat, half cover the pan and simmer gently for 20 minutes, stirring occasionally to stop the tomatoes sticking to the base of the pan.

3 ▲ Process the soup with the shredded basil in a blender or food processor, then press through a sieve (strainer) into a clean pan.

4 ▲ Add the double cream and heat through, stirring. Do not allow the soup to approach boiling point. Check the consistency and add more stock if necessary and then taste for seasoning. Pour into heated bowls and garnish with basil. Serve at once.

Variation

The soup can also be served chilled. Pour it into a container after sieving (straining) and chill for at least 4 hours. Serve in chilled bowls.

Minestrone with Pasta and Beans

Minestrone alla milanese

This classic minestrone from Lombardy includes pancetta for a pleasant touch of saltiness. Milanese cooks vary the recipe according to what is on hand, and you can do the same.

Ingredients

45 ml/3 tbsp olive oil
115 g/4 oz pancetta, any rinds removed, roughly chopped
2–3 celery sticks, finely chopped
3 medium carrots, finely chopped
1 medium onion, finely chopped
1–2 garlic cloves, crushed
2 x 400 g/14 oz cans chopped tomatoes
1 litre/1¾ pints/4 cups chicken stock
400 g/14 oz can cannellini beans, drained and rinsed
50 g/2 oz/½ cup short-cut macaroni
30–60 ml/2–4 tbsp chopped flat leaf parsley, to taste
salt and freshly ground black pepper
shaved Parmesan cheese, to serve
serves 4

Variation

Use long-grain rice instead of the pasta, and borlotti beans instead of cannellini.

1 ▲ Heat the oil in a large pan. Add the pancetta, celery, carrots and onion and cook over a low heat for 5 minutes, stirring constantly, until the vegetables are softened.

2 Add the garlic and tomatoes, breaking them up well with a wooden spoon. Pour in the stock. Add salt and pepper to taste and bring to the boil. Half cover the pan, lower the heat and simmer gently for about 20 minutes, until the vegetables are soft.

3 ▲ Drain the beans and add them to the pan with the macaroni. Bring to the boil again. Cover, lower the heat and continue to simmer for about 20 minutes more. Check the consistency and add more stock if necessary. Stir in the parsley and taste for seasoning.

4 Serve hot, sprinkled with plenty of Parmesan cheese. This makes a meal in itself if served with chunks of crusty Italian bread.

Summer Minestrone

Minestrone estivo

This brightly coloured, fresh-tasting soup makes the most of summer vegetables.

Ingredients

45 ml/3 tbsp olive oil
1 large onion, finely chopped
15 ml/1 tbsp sun-dried tomato paste
450 g/1 lb ripe Italian plum tomatoes, peeled and finely chopped
225 g/8 oz green courgettes, trimmed and roughly chopped
225 g/8 oz yellow courgettes (zucchini), trimmed and roughly chopped
3 waxy new potatoes, diced
2 garlic cloves, crushed
1.2 litres/2 pints/5 cups chicken stock or water
60 ml/4 tbsp shredded fresh basil
50 g/2 oz/⅔ cup grated Parmesan cheese
salt and freshly ground black pepper
serves 4

1 ▲ Heat the oil in a large pan, add the onion and cook gently for about 5 minutes, stirring constantly, until softened. Stir in the sun-dried tomato paste, chopped tomatoes, courgettes, diced potatoes and garlic. Mix well and cook gently for 10 minutes, uncovered, shaking the pan frequently to stop the vegetables sticking to the base.

2 ▲ Pour in the stock. Bring to the boil, lower the heat, half cover the pan and simmer gently for 15 minutes or until the vegetables are just tender. Add more stock if necessary.

3 Remove the pan from the heat and stir in the basil and half the cheese. Taste for seasoning. Serve hot, sprinkled with the remaining cheese.

Clam and Pasta Soup

Zuppa alle vongole

This soup is a play on the pasta dish – spaghetti alle vongole – using store cupboard ingredients. Serve it with hot focaccia or ciabatta for an informal supper with friends.

Ingredients
30 ml/2 tbsp olive oil
1 large onion, finely chopped
2 garlic cloves, crushed
400 g/14 oz can chopped tomatoes
15 ml/1 tbsp sun-dried tomato paste
5 ml/1 tsp sugar
5 ml/1 tsp dried mixed herbs
about 750 ml/1¼ pints/3 cups fish or vegetable stock
150 ml/¼ pint/⅔ cup red wine
50 g/2 oz/½ cup small pasta shapes
150 g/5 oz jar or can clams in natural juice
30 ml/2 tbsp finely chopped flat leaf parsley, plus a few whole leaves, to garnish
salt and freshly ground black pepper
serves 4

1 ▲ Heat the oil in a large pan. Cook the onion gently for 5 minutes, stirring frequently, until softened.

2 ▲ Add the garlic, tomatoes, tomato paste, sugar, herbs, stock and wine, with salt and pepper to taste. Bring to the boil. Lower the heat, half cover the pan and simmer for 10 minutes, stirring occasionally.

3 ▲ Add the pasta and continue simmering, uncovered, for about 10 minutes or until *al dente*. Stir occasionally, to prevent the pasta shapes from sticking together.

Cook's Tip
This soup has a fuller flavour if it is made the day before and reheated.

4 ▲ Add the clams and their juice to the soup and heat through for 3–4 minutes, adding more stock if required. Do not let it boil or the clams will be tough. Remove from the heat, stir in the parsley and taste the soup for seasoning. Serve hot, sprinkled with coarsely ground black pepper and parsley leaves.

Tuscan Bean Soup

Zuppa di fagioli alla toscana

There are lots of versions of this wonderful soup. This one uses cannellini beans, leeks, cabbage and good olive oil – and tastes even better reheated.

Ingredients
45 ml/3 tbsp extra virgin olive oil
1 onion, roughly chopped
2 leeks, roughly chopped
1 large potato, peeled and diced
2 garlic cloves, finely chopped
1.2 litres/2 pints/5 cups vegetable stock
400 g/14 oz can cannellini beans, drained, liquid reserved
175 g/6 oz Savoy cabbage, shredded
45 ml/3 tbsp chopped fresh flat leaf parsley
30 ml/2 tbsp chopped fresh oregano
75 g/3 oz/1 cup Parmesan cheese, shaved
salt and freshly ground black pepper

For the garlic toasts
30–45 ml/2–3 tbsp extra virgin olive oil
6 thick slices country bread
1 garlic clove, peeled and bruised
serves 4

1 ▲ Heat the oil in a large pan and gently cook the onion, leeks, potato and garlic for 4–5 minutes.

2 ▲ Pour on the stock and liquid from the beans. Cover and simmer for 15 minutes.

3 ▲ Stir in the cabbage and beans, with half the herbs, season and cook for 10 minutes more. Spoon about one-third of the soup into a food processor or blender and process until fairly smooth. Return to the soup in the pan, taste for seasoning and heat through for 5 minutes.

4 ▲ Meanwhile make the garlic toasts. Drizzle a little oil over the slices of bread, then rub both sides of each slice with the garlic. Toast until browned on both sides. Ladle the soup into bowls. Sprinkle with the remaining herbs and the Parmesan shavings. Add a drizzle of olive oil and serve with the toasts.

Salad Leaves with Gorgonzola

Insalata verde con gorgonzola

Crispy fried pancetta makes tasty croûtons, which contrast well in texture and flavour with the softness of mixed salad leaves and the sharp taste of Gorgonzola.

Ingredients

225 g/8 oz pancetta rashers, any rinds removed, coarsely chopped
2 large garlic cloves, roughly chopped
75 g/3 oz rocket (arugula) leaves
75 g/3 oz radicchio leaves
50 g/2 oz/½ cup walnuts, roughly chopped
115 g/4 oz Gorgonzola cheese
60 ml/4 tbsp olive oil
15 ml/1 tbsp balsamic vinegar
salt and freshly ground black pepper
serves 4

Variation

Use walnut oil instead of olive oil, or hazelnuts and hazelnut oil instead of walnuts and olive oil.

1 ▲ Put the chopped pancetta and garlic in a non-stick or heavy-based frying pan and heat gently, stirring constantly, until the pancetta fat runs. Increase the heat and fry until the pancetta and garlic are crisp. Remove with a slotted spoon and drain on kitchen paper. Leave the pancetta fat in the pan, off the heat.

2 ▲ Tear the rocket and radicchio leaves into a salad bowl. Sprinkle over the walnuts, pancetta and garlic. Add salt and pepper and toss to mix. Crumble the Gorgonzola on top.

3 Return the frying pan to a medium heat and add the oil and balsamic vinegar to the pancetta fat. Stir until sizzling, then pour over the salad. Serve at once, to be tossed at the table.

Tomato and Mozzarella Toasts

Bruschetta casalinga

These resemble mini pizzas and are good with drinks before a dinner party. Prepare them several hours in advance and pop them in the oven just as your guests arrive.

Ingredients

3 *sfilatini* (thin ciabatta)
about 250 ml/8 fl oz/1 cup sun-dried tomato paste
3 x 150 g/5 oz packets mozzarella cheese, drained
about 10 ml/2 tsp dried oregano or mixed herbs
30–45 ml/2–3 tbsp olive oil
freshly ground black pepper
serves 6–8

Variations

Use red or green pesto instead of the sun-dried tomato paste – a combination of colours is especially effective if the toasts are served on a large platter. Halved olives can be pressed into the cheese, or criss-cross strips of anchovy.

1 ▲ Cut each *sfilatino* on the diagonal into 12–15 slices, discarding the ends. Toast lightly on both sides.

2 Preheat the oven to 220°C/425°F/Gas 7. Spread sun-dried tomato paste on one side of each slice of toast. Cut the mozzarella into small pieces and arrange over the tomato paste.

3 ▲ Put the toasts on baking sheets, sprinkle with herbs and pepper to taste and drizzle with oil. Bake for 5 minutes or until the mozzarella has melted and is bubbling. Leave the toasts to settle for a few minutes before serving.

Marinated Vegetable Antipasto

Verdura marinata per antipasto

Antipasto means "before the meal" and traditionally consists of a selection of marinated vegetable dishes served with good Italian salami and thin slices of Parma ham. Serve in attractive bowls, with plenty of fresh crusty bread.

Ingredients

For the peppers

3 red (bell) peppers
3 yellow (bell) peppers
4 garlic cloves, sliced
handful fresh basil, plus extra to garnish
extra virgin olive oil
salt and freshly ground black pepper

For the mushrooms

450 g/1 lb open cap mushrooms
60 ml/4 tbsp extra virgin olive oil
1 large garlic clove, crushed
15 ml/1 tbsp chopped fresh rosemary
250 ml/8 fl oz/1 cup dry white wine
fresh rosemary sprigs, to garnish

For the olives

1 dried red chilli, crushed
grated rind of 1 lemon
120 ml/4 fl oz/½ cup extra virgin olive oil
225 g/8 oz/1⅓ cups Italian black olives
30 ml/2 tbsp chopped fresh flat leaf parsley
1 lemon wedge, to serve

serves 4

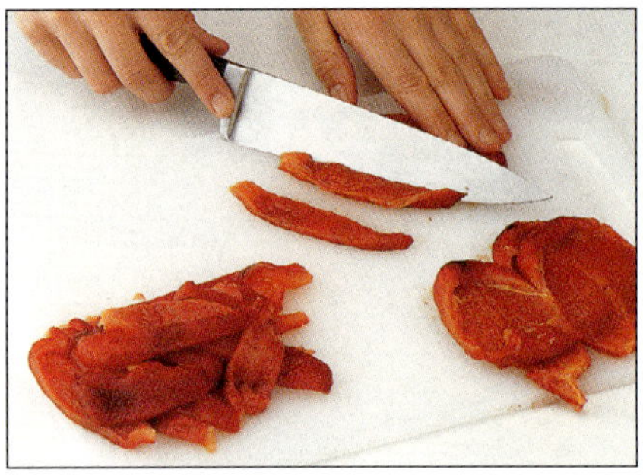

1 ▲ Place the peppers under a hot grill (broiler). Turn occasionally until they are blackened and blistered all over. Remove from the heat and place in a large plastic bag. When cool, remove the skin, halve the peppers and remove the seeds. Cut the flesh into strips lengthways and place them in a bowl with the sliced garlic and basil leaves. Add salt, to taste, cover with oil and marinate for 3–4 hours before serving, tossing occasionally. When serving garnish with more basil leaves.

3 Thickly slice the mushrooms and place in a large bowl. Heat the oil in a small pan and add the garlic and rosemary. Pour in the wine. Bring the mixture to the boil, then lower the heat and simmer for 3 minutes. Add salt and pepper to taste.

4 ▲ Pour the mixture over the mushrooms. Mix well and leave until cool, stirring occasionally. Cover and marinate overnight. Serve at room temperature, garnished with rosemary sprigs.

5 ▲ Prepare the olives. Place the chilli and lemon rind in a small pan with the oil. Heat gently for about 3 minutes. Add the olives and heat for 1 minute more. Tip into a bowl and leave to cool. Marinate overnight. Sprinkle the parsley over just before serving with the lemon wedge.

Cook's Tip

The pepper antipasto can be stored in the refrigerator for up to 2 weeks covered in olive oil in a screw-top jar.

Stuffed Roast Peppers with Pesto

Peperoni arrostiti con pesto

Serve these scallop- and pesto-filled sweet red peppers with freshly baked Italian bread, such as ciabatta or focaccia, to mop up the garlicky juices.

Ingredients
4 squat red (bell) peppers
2 large garlic cloves, cut into thin slivers
60 ml/4 tbsp olive oil
4 shelled scallops
45 ml/3 tbsp pesto
salt and freshly ground black pepper
freshly grated Parmesan cheese, to serve
salad leaves and fresh basil sprigs, to garnish
serves 4

Cook's Tip

Scallops are available from most fishmongers and supermarkets with fresh fish counters. Never cook scallops for longer than the time stated in the recipe or they will be tough and rubbery.

1 Preheat the oven to 180°C/350°F/Gas 4. Cut the peppers in half lengthways, through their stalks. Scrape out and discard the cores and seeds. Wash the pepper shells and pat dry.

2 ▲ Put the peppers, cut-side up, in an oiled roasting pan. Divide the slivers of garlic equally among them and sprinkle with salt and pepper to taste. Spoon the oil into the peppers, then roast for 40 minutes.

3 ▲ Cut each of the shelled scallops in half to make two flat discs. Remove the peppers from the oven and place a scallop half in each pepper half. Top with pesto.

4 Return the pan to the oven and roast for 10 minutes more. Transfer the peppers to individual serving plates, sprinkle with grated Parmesan and garnish each plate with a few salad leaves and fresh basil sprigs. Serve warm.

Mozzarella Skewers

Spiedini alla romana

Stacks of flavour – layers of oven-baked mozzarella, tomatoes, basil and bread.

Ingredients

12 slices white country bread, each about 1 cm/½ in thick
45 ml/3 tbsp olive oil
225 g/8 oz mozzarella cheese, cut into 5 mm/¼ in slices
3 plum tomatoes, cut into 5 mm/¼ in slices
15 g/½ oz/½ cup fresh basil leaves, plus extra to garnish
salt and freshly ground black pepper
30 ml/2 tbsp chopped fresh flat leaf parsley, to garnish
serves 4

Cook's Tip

If you use wooden skewers, soak them in water first, to prevent scorching.

1 ▲ Preheat the oven to 220°C/425°F/Gas 7. Trim the crusts from the bread and cut each slice into four equal squares. Arrange on a baking sheet and brush on one side (or both sides) with half the olive oil. Bake for 3–5 minutes until the squares are pale golden.

2 Remove from the oven and place the bread squares on a board with the other ingredients.

3 ▲ Make 16 stacks, each starting with a square of bread, then a slice of mozzarella topped with a slice of tomato and a basil leaf. Sprinkle with salt and pepper, then repeat, ending with the bread. Push a skewer through each stack and place on the baking sheet. Drizzle with the remaining oil and bake for 10–15 minutes until the cheese begins to melt. Garnish with fresh basil leaves and serve sprinkled with chopped fresh flat leaf parsley.

Aubergine Fritters

Frittelle di melanzane

These simply delicious fritters make a superb appetizer or vegetarian supper dish.

Ingredients

1 large aubergine (eggplant), about 675 g/1½ lb, cut into 1 cm/½ in thick slices
30 ml/2 tbsp olive oil
1 egg, lightly beaten
2 garlic cloves, crushed
60 ml/4 tbsp chopped fresh parsley
130 g/4½ oz/2¼ cups fresh white breadcrumbs
90 g/3½ oz/generous 1 cup grated Parmesan cheese
90 g/3½ oz/generous 1 cup feta cheese, crumbled
45 ml/3 tbsp plain (all-purpose) flour
sunflower oil, for shallow frying
salt and freshly ground black pepper

To serve

natural (plain) yogurt, flavoured with fried red chillies and cumin seeds
lime wedges
serves 4

1 ▲ Preheat the oven to 190°C/375°F/Gas 5. Brush the aubergine slices with the olive oil, then place them on a baking sheet and bake for about 20 minutes until golden and tender. Chop the slices finely and place them in a bowl with the egg, garlic, parsley, breadcrumbs, Parmesan and feta. Add salt and pepper to taste, and mix well. Leave the mixture to rest for about 20 minutes. If the mixture looks very sloppy, add more breadcrumbs.

2 ▲ Divide the mixture into eight balls and flatten them slightly. Place the flour on a plate and season with salt and pepper. Coat the fritters in the flour, shaking off any excess.

3 Shallow fry the fritters in batches for 1 minute on each side, until golden brown. Drain on kitchen paper and serve with the flavoured yogurt and lime wedges.

Vegetables and Salads

There is no shortage of fresh and delicious vegetables in Italy, and the dishes are imaginative and varied. Most Italian cooks buy only when the vegetables are in season and at their best, so you will rarely find winter and summer vegetables together in one dish. The list of irresistible salad combinations is endless, often with roasted ingredients stirred into crisp green leaves.

Roasted Plum Tomatoes and Garlic

Pomodori al forno

These are so simple to prepare, yet taste absolutely wonderful. Use a large, shallow earthenware dish that will allow the tomatoes to sear and char in a hot oven.

Ingredients

8 plum tomatoes, halved
12 garlic cloves
60 ml/4 tbsp extra virgin olive oil
3 bay leaves
salt and freshly ground black pepper
45 ml/3 tbsp fresh oregano leaves, to garnish

serves 4

Cook's Tip

Use ripe plum tomatoes for this recipe as they keep their shape and do not fall apart when roasted at such a high temperature. Leave the stalks on, if possible.

1 ▲ Preheat the oven to 230°C/450°F/ Gas 8. Select an ovenproof dish that will hold all the tomatoes snugly in a single layer. Place the tomatoes in the dish and push the whole, unpeeled garlic cloves between them.

2 ▲ Brush the tomatoes with the oil, add the bay leaves and sprinkle black pepper over the top. Bake for about 45 minutes until the tomatoes have softened and are sizzling in the pan. They should be charred around the edges. Season with salt and a little more black pepper, if needed. Garnish with oregano and serve.

Green Beans with Tomatoes

Fagiolini al pomodoro

This is a real summer favourite using the best ripe plum tomatoes and Green beans.

Ingredients

30 ml/2 tbsp olive oil
1 large onion, finely sliced
2 garlic cloves, finely chopped
6 large ripe plum tomatoes, peeled, seeded and coarsely chopped
150 ml/¼ pint/⅔ cup dry white wine
450 g/1 lb green beans, sliced in half lengthways
16 pitted black olives
10 ml/2 tsp lemon juice
salt and freshly ground black pepper

serves 4

Cook's Tip

Green beans need little preparation and now that they are grown without the string you simply top and tail them. When choosing make sure that the beans snap easily - this is a good sign of freshness.

1 ▲ Heat the oil in a large frying pan. Add the onion and garlic and cook for about 5 minutes until the onion is softened but not brown.

2 ▲ Add the chopped tomatoes, white wine, beans, olives and lemon juice and cook over a gentle heat for a further 20 minutes, stirring from time to time, until the sauce is thickened and the beans are tender. Season with salt and pepper to taste and serve at once.

Fennel Gratin

Finocchi gratinati

This is one of the best ways to eat fresh fennel. The fennel takes on a delicious, almost creamy, flavour, which contrasts beautifully with the sharp, strong Gruyère.

Ingredients
- 2 fennel bulbs, about 675 g/1½ lb total weight
- 300 ml/½ pint/1¼ cups milk
- 15 g/½ oz/1 tbsp butter, plus extra for greasing
- 15 ml/1 tbsp plain (all-purpose) flour
- 75 g/3 oz Gruyère cheese, grated
- 25 g/1 oz/scant ½ cup dry white breadcrumbs
- salt and freshly ground black pepper

serves 4

Cook's Tip
Instead of the Gruyère, Parmesan, Pecorino or any other strong cheese would work perfectly.

1 ▲ Preheat the oven to 240°C/475°F/Gas 9. Discard the stalks and root ends from the fennel. Slice into quarters and place in a large pan. Pour over the milk and simmer for 10–15 minutes until tender. Butter a small baking dish.

2 Remove the fennel pieces with a slotted spoon, reserving the milk and arrange the fennel pieces in the dish.

3 ▲ Melt the butter in a small saucepan and add the flour, stir well, then gradually whisk in the reserved milk. Stir the sauce until thickened.

4 Pour the sauce over the fennel pieces, sprinkle with the white breadcrumbs and grated Gruyère. Season with salt and black pepper and bake for about 20 minutes until browned.

Sweet and Sour Onions

Cipolline in agrodolce

Onions are naturally sweet, and when they are cooked at a high temperature the sweetness intensifies. Serve with roasts and meat dishes or as part of an antipasti.

Ingredients
- 50 g/2 oz/¼ cup butter
- 75 ml/5 tbsp sugar
- 120 ml/4 fl oz/½ cup white wine vinegar
- 30 ml/2 tbsp balsamic vinegar
- 675 g/1½ lb small pickling onions, peeled
- salt and freshly ground black pepper

serves 4

Cook's Tips
This recipe also looks and tastes delicious when made with either yellow or red onions, which are cut into either thin slices or into chunks. Cooking times will vary, depending on the size of the onion pieces.

1 ▲ Heat the butter in a large pan over a gentle heat. Add the sugar and heat until dissolved, stirring constantly.

2 ▲ Add the vinegars to the pan with the onions and mix together well. Season with salt and pepper and cover and cook over a medium heat for 20–25 minutes until the onions are a golden colour and soft when pierced with a knife. Serve hot.

Roasted Potatoes with Red Onions

Patate al forno

These mouth-watering potatoes are a fine accompaniment to just about anything. The key is to use small firm potatoes; the smaller they are cut, the quicker they will cook.

Ingredients

675 g/1½ lb small firm potatoes
25 g/1 oz/2 tbsp butter
30 ml/2 tbsp olive oil
2 red onions, cut into chunks
8 garlic cloves, unpeeled
30 ml/2 tbsp chopped fresh rosemary
salt and freshly ground black pepper
serves 4

Cook's Tip

To ensure that the potatoes are crisp, make sure they are completely dry before cooking. Resist the urge to turn the potatoes too often. Allow them to brown on one side before turning. Do not salt the potatoes until the end of cooking – salting beforehand encourages them to give up their liquid, making them limp.

1 ▲ Preheat the oven to 230°C/450°F/ Gas 8. Peel and quarter the potatoes, rinse them well and pat thoroughly dry on kitchen paper. Place the butter and oil in a roasting pan and place in the oven to heat.

2 ▲ When the butter has melted and is foaming, add the potatoes, red onions, garlic and rosemary. Toss well then spread out in one layer.

3 Place the pan in the oven and roast for about 25 minutes until the potatoes are golden and tender when tested with a fork. Shake the pan from time to time to redistribute the potatoes. When cooked, season with salt and pepper.

Radicchio and Chicory Gratin

Radicchio e indivia gratinati

Vegetables like radicchio and chicory take on a different flavour when cooked in this way. The creamy béchamel combines wonderfully with the bitter leaves.

Ingredients
2 heads radicchio, quartered
2 heads chicory (Belgian endive), quartered
25 g/1 oz/½ cup drained sun-dried tomatoes in oil, chopped roughly
25 g/1 oz/2 tbsp butter
15 g/½ oz/1 tbsp plain (all-purpose) flour
250 ml/8 fl oz/1 cup milk
pinch grated nutmeg
50 g/2 oz/½ cup grated Emmenthal cheese
salt and freshly ground black pepper
chopped fresh parsley, to garnish
serves 4

1 ▲ Preheat the oven to 180°C/350°F/ Gas 4. Grease a 1.2 litre/2 pint/5 cup baking dish. Trim the radicchio and chicory and pull away any damaged or wilted leaves. Quarter them lengthways and arrange in the baking dish.

2 Scatter the sun-dried tomatoes over the radicchio and chicory and brush the leaves liberally with the oil from the jar. Sprinkle with salt and pepper and cover with foil. Bake for 15 minutes, then remove the foil and bake for a further 10 minutes until soft.

Cook's Tip
In Italy radicchio and chicory are often cooked on a barbecue. To do this, simply prepare the vegetables as above and brush with olive oil. Place cut-side down on the barbecue for 7–10 minutes until browned. Turn and cook until the other side is browned, about 5 minutes longer.

3 ▲ Make the sauce. Place the butter in a small pan and melt over a moderate heat. When the butter is foaming, add the flour and cook for 1 minute, stirring. Remove from the heat and gradually add the milk, whisking all the time. Return to the heat and bring to the boil, simmer for 2–3 minutes to thicken. Season to taste and add the nutmeg.

4 Pour the sauce over the vegetables and sprinkle with the grated cheese. Bake for about 20 minutes until golden. Serve immediately, garnished with parsley.

Fennel, Orange and Rocket Salad

Insalata di finocchio

This light and refreshing salad is ideal to serve with spicy or rich foods.

Ingredients
2 oranges
1 fennel bulb
115 g/4 oz rocket (arugula) leaves
50 g/2 oz/⅓ cup black olives

For the dressing
30 ml/2 tbsp extra virgin olive oil
15 ml/1 tbsp balsamic vinegar
1 small garlic clove, crushed
salt and freshly ground black pepper
serves 4

1 With a vegetable peeler, cut strips of rind from the oranges, leaving the pith behind, and cut into thin julienne strips. Cook in boiling water for a few minutes. Drain. Peel the oranges, removing all the white pith. Slice them into thin rounds and discard any seeds.

2 Cut the fennel bulb in half lengthways and slice across the bulb as thinly as possible, preferably in a food processor fitted with a slicing disc or using a mandoline.

3 ▲ Combine the oranges and fennel in a serving bowl and toss with the rocket leaves.

4 ▲ Mix together the oil, vinegar, garlic and seasoning and pour over the salad, toss together well and leave to stand for a few minutes. Sprinkle with the black olives and julienne strips of orange rind.

Aubergine, Lemon and Caper Salad

Caponata

This cooked vegetable relish is a classic Sicilian dish, which is delicious served as an accompaniment to cold meats, with pasta or simply on its own with some good crusty bread. Make sure the aubergine is well cooked until it is meltingly soft.

Ingredients
1 large aubergine (eggplant), about 675 g/1½ lb
60 ml/4 tbsp olive oil
grated rind and juice of 1 lemon
30 ml/2 tbsp capers, rinsed
12 stoned green olives
30 ml/2 tbsp chopped fresh flat leaf parsley
salt and freshly ground black pepper
serves 4

Cook's Tips
This will taste even better when made the day before. Serve at room temperature. It will store, covered in the fridge, for up to 4 days. To enrich this dish to serve it on its own as a main course, add toasted pine nuts and shavings of Parmesan cheese. Serve with crusty bread.

1 ▲ Cut the aubergine into 2.5 cm/1 in cubes. Heat the olive oil in a large frying pan and cook the aubergine cubes over a medium heat for about 10 minutes, tossing regularly, until golden and softened. You may need to do this in two batches. Drain on kitchen paper and sprinkle with a little salt.

2 ▲ Place the aubergine cubes in a large serving bowl, toss with the lemon rind and juice, capers, olives and chopped parsley and season well with salt and pepper. Serve at room temperature.

Spinach and Roast Garlic Salad

Insalata di spinaci con aglio arrosto

Don't worry about the amount of garlic in this salad. During roasting, the garlic becomes aromatic, sweet and subtle and loses its overpowering pungent taste.

Ingredients

12 garlic cloves, unpeeled
60 ml/4 tbsp extra virgin olive oil
450 g/1 lb baby spinach leaves
50 g/2 oz/½ cup pine nuts, lightly toasted
juice of ½ lemon
salt and freshly ground black pepper
serves 4

Cook's Tip

If spinach is to be served raw in a salad, the leaves need to be young and tender. Wash them well, drain and pat dry with kitchen paper.

1 ▲ Preheat the oven to 190°C/375°F/Gas 5. Place the garlic in a small roasting dish, toss in 30 ml/2 tbsp of the olive oil and bake for about 15 minutes until the garlic cloves are slightly charred around the edges.

2 ▲ While still warm, tip the garlic into a salad bowl. Add the spinach, pine nuts, lemon juice, remaining olive oil and a little salt. Toss well and add black pepper to taste. Serve immediately, inviting guests to squeeze the softened garlic purée out of the skin to eat.

Sweet and Sour Artichoke Salad

Carciofi in salsa agrodolce

Agrodolce is a sweet and sour sauce which works perfectly in this salad.

Ingredients
6 small globe artichokes
juice of 1 lemon
30 ml/2 tbsp olive oil
2 medium onions, roughly chopped
175 g/6 oz/1 cup fresh or frozen broad (fava) beans (shelled weight)
175 g/6 oz/1½ cups fresh or frozen peas (shelled weight)
salt and freshly ground black pepper
fresh mint leaves, to garnish

For the salsa agrodolce
120 ml/4 fl oz/½ cup white wine vinegar
15 ml/1 tbsp caster (superfine) sugar
handful fresh mint leaves, roughly torn
serves 4

1 ▲ Peel the outer leaves from the artichokes and cut into quarters. Place the artichokes in a bowl of water with the lemon juice.

2 ▲ Heat the oil in a large saucepan and add the onions. Cook until the onions are golden. Add the beans and stir, then drain the artichokes and add to the pan. Pour in about 300 ml/½ pint/1¼ cups of water and cook, covered, for 10–15 minutes.

3 ▲ Add the peas, season with salt and pepper and cook for a further 5 minutes, stirring from time to time, until the vegetables are tender. Strain through a sieve (strainer) and place all the vegetables in a bowl, leave to cool, then cover and chill.

4 ▲ To make the salsa agrodolce, mix all the ingredients in a small pan. Heat gently for 2–3 minutes until the sugar has dissolved. Simmer gently for about 5 minutes, stirring occasionally. Leave to cool. To serve, drizzle the salsa over the vegetables and garnish with mint leaves.

Roasted Pepper and Tomato Salad

Peperoni arrostiti con pomodori

This is one of those lovely recipes which brings together perfectly the colours, flavours and textures of southern Italian food. Eat this dish at room temperature with a green salad.

Ingredients
3 red (bell) peppers
6 large plum tomatoes
2.5 ml/½ tsp dried red chilli flakes
1 red onion, finely sliced
3 garlic cloves, finely chopped
grated rind and juice of 1 lemon
45 ml/3 tbsp chopped fresh flat leaf parsley
30 ml/2 tbsp extra virgin olive oil
salt and freshly ground black pepper
black and green olives and extra chopped flat leaf parsley, to garnish
serves 4

Cook's Tip
Peppers roasted this way will keep for several weeks. After peeling off the skins, place the pepper pieces in a jar with a tight-fitting lid. Pour enough olive oil over them to cover completely. Store in the refrigerator.

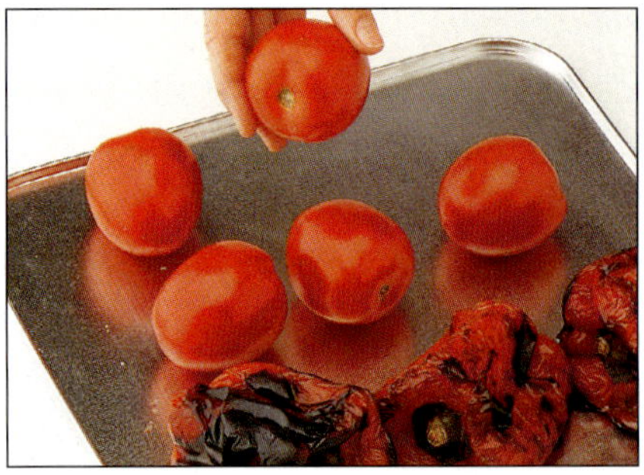

1 ▲ Preheat the oven to 220°C/425°F/ Gas 7. Place the peppers on a baking sheet and roast, turning occasionally, for 10 minutes or until the skins are almost blackened. Add the tomatoes to the baking sheet and bake for 5 minutes more.

2 Place the peppers in a plastic bag, close the top loosely, trapping in the steam, and then set them aside, with the tomatoes, until they are cool enough to handle.

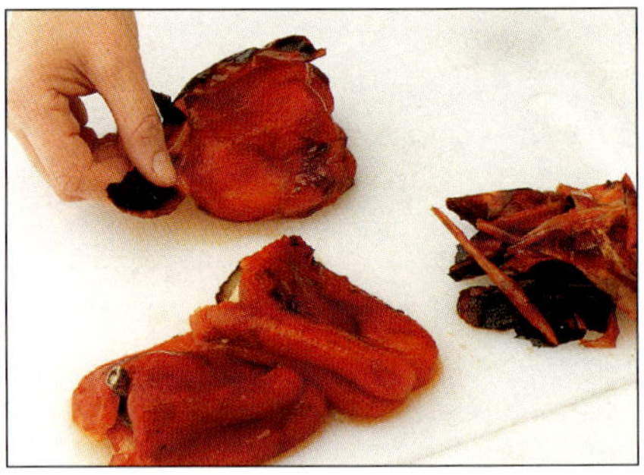

3 ▲ Carefully pull off the skin from the peppers. Remove the seeds, then chop the peppers and tomatoes roughly and place in a mixing bowl.

4 Add the chilli flakes, onion, garlic, lemon rind and juice. Sprinkle over the parsley. Mix well, then transfer to a serving dish. Sprinkle with a little salt, drizzle over the olive oil and scatter olives and extra parsley over the top. Serve at room temperature.

Marinated Courgettes

Zucchini a scapece

This is a simple, yet delicious, vegetable dish which is prepared all over Italy using the best of the season's courgettes. It can be eaten hot or cold.

Ingredients
4 courgettes (zucchini)
60 ml/4 tbsp extra virgin olive oil
30 ml/2 tbsp chopped fresh mint, plus whole leaves, to garnish
30 ml/2 tbsp white wine vinegar
salt and freshly ground black pepper
wholemeal (whole-wheat) Italian bread and green olives, to serve
serves 4

Cook's Tip
Carrots, onions or green beans can also be prepared in this way.

1 ▲ Cut the courgettes into thin slices. Heat 30 ml/2 tbsp of the oil in a wide heavy-based pan. Fry the courgettes in batches, for 4–6 minutes, until tender and brown around the edges. Transfer the courgettes to a bowl. Season well.

2 ▲ Heat the remaining oil in the pan, then add the mint and vinegar and let it bubble for a few seconds. Pour over the courgettes. Marinate for 1 hour, then serve garnished with mint and accompanied by bread and olives.

Pasta and Gnocchi

In Italy, pasta and gnocchi are traditionally served as first courses after the antipasti and before the second course of fish or meat. Everyday dishes are often simple, served with nothing more than olive oil or butter, grated Parmesan and basil. Outside of Italy there are no hard-and-fast rules, and nowadays people eat pasta and gnocchi dishes whenever they like.

Cannelloni with Tuna

Cannelloni sorpresa

Children love this pasta dish. Fontina cheese has a sweet, nutty flavour and very good melting qualities. Look for it in large supermarkets and Italian delicatessens.

Ingredients

50 g/2 oz/¼ cup butter
50 g/2 oz/½ cup plain (all-purpose) flour
about 900 ml/1½ pints/3 ¾ cups hot milk
2 x 200 g/7 oz cans tuna, drained
115 g/4 oz/1 cup Fontina cheese, grated
1.5 ml/¼ tsp grated nutmeg
12 no-precook cannelloni tubes
50 g/2 oz/⅔ cup grated Parmesan cheese
salt and freshly ground black pepper
fresh herbs, to garnish

serves 4–6

1 ▲ Melt the butter in a heavy-based pan, add the flour and stir over a low heat for 1–2 minutes. Remove the pan from the heat and gradually add 350 ml/12 fl oz/1½ cups of the milk, beating vigorously after each addition. Return the pan to the heat and whisk for 1–2 minutes until the sauce is very thick and smooth. Remove from the heat.

2 ▲ Mix the drained tuna with about 120 ml/4 fl oz/½ cup of the warm white sauce in a bowl. Add salt and black pepper to taste. Preheat the oven to 180°C/350°F/Gas 4.

3 ▲ Gradually whisk the remaining milk into the rest of the sauce, then return to the heat and simmer, whisking constantly, until thickened. Add the grated Fontina and nutmeg, with salt and pepper to taste. Simmer for a few more minutes, stirring frequently. Pour about one-third of the sauce into a baking dish and spread to the corners.

4 ▲ Fill the cannelloni tubes with the tuna mixture, pushing it in with the handle of a teaspoon. Place the cannelloni in a single layer in the dish. Thin the remaining sauce with a little more milk if necessary, then pour it over the cannelloni. Sprinkle with Parmesan cheese and bake for 30 minutes or until golden. Serve hot, garnished with herbs.

Seafood Lasagne

Lasagne alla marinara

Rich and creamy, this flavoursome lasagne makes a good supper-party dish.

Ingredients

65 g/2 ½ oz/5 tbsp butter
450 g/1 lb monkfish fillets, skinned and diced small
225 g/8 oz fresh prawns (large shrimp), shelled, deveined and roughly chopped
225 g/8 oz/3 cups mushrooms, chopped
40 g/1½ oz/3 tbsp plain (all-purpose) flour
600 ml/1 pint/2 ½ cups hot milk
300 ml/½ pint/1¼ cups double (heavy) cream
400 g/14 oz can chopped tomatoes
30 ml/2 tbsp shredded fresh basil
8 sheets no-precook lasagne
75 g/3 oz/1 cup grated Parmesan cheese
salt and freshly ground black pepper
fresh herbs, to garnish

serves 6

1 ▲ Melt 15 g/½ oz/1 tbsp of the butter in a large, deep sauté pan, add the monkfish and prawns and sauté over a medium to high heat for 2–3 minutes. As soon as the prawns turn pink, remove them with a slotted spoon and place in a bowl.

2 Add the mushrooms to the pan and sauté for about 5 minutes until the juices run and the mushrooms are soft. Remove with a slotted spoon and add to the fish in the bowl.

3 Melt the remaining butter in a saucepan, add the flour and stir over a low heat for 1–2 minutes. Remove the pan from the heat and gradually whisk in the milk. Return to the heat and bring to the boil, whisking. Lower the heat and simmer for 2–3 minutes, whisking occasionally, until thick. Whisk in the cream and cook over a low heat for 2 minutes more.

4 ▲ Remove the sauce from the heat and stir in the fish and mushroom mixture with all the juices that have collected in the bowl. Add salt to taste, and plenty of pepper. Preheat the oven to 190°C/375°F/Gas 5.

5 Spread half the chopped tomatoes over the bottom of a baking dish. Sprinkle with half the basil and add salt and pepper to taste. Ladle one-third of the sauce over the tomatoes.

6 ▲ Cover the sauce with four lasagne sheets. Spread the remaining tomatoes over the lasagne and sprinkle with the remaining basil and salt and pepper to taste. Ladle half the remaining sauce over. Arrange the remaining lasagne sheets on top, top with the remaining sauce and cover with the cheese. Bake for 30–40 minutes until golden and bubbling. Serve hot, garnished with fresh herbs.

Spaghetti with Clams and White Wine

Spaghetti alle vongole

Raid the pantry to make this quick and easy pasta dish with an intense flavour.

Ingredients
30 ml/2 tbsp olive oil
1 onion, very finely chopped
2 garlic cloves, crushed
400 g/14 oz can chopped tomatoes
150 ml/¼ pint/⅔ cup dry white wine
150 g/5 oz jar or can clams in natural juice, drained with juice reserved
350 g/12 oz dried spaghetti
30 ml/2 tbsp finely chopped fresh flat leaf parsley, plus extra to garnish
salt and freshly ground black pepper
serves 4

Cook's Tip
The tomato sauce can be made several days ahead of time and kept in the fridge. Add the clams and heat them through at the last minute - but don't let them boil or they will toughen.

1 Heat the oil in a heavy pan, add the onion and cook gently, stirring frequently, for about 5 minutes until softened, but not brown.

2 ▲ Stir in the garlic, tomatoes, wine and reserved clam juice, with salt to taste. Add a generous grinding of black pepper. Bring to the boil, stirring, then lower the heat. Cover the pan and simmer the sauce gently for about 20 minutes, stirring from time to time.

3 ▲ Meanwhile, coil the spaghetti into a large pan of rapidly boiling salted water and cook for 12 minutes or until it is *al dente*.

4 Drain the spaghetti thoroughly. Add the clams and finely chopped parsley to the tomato sauce and heat through, then taste for seasoning. Tip the drained spaghetti into a warmed serving bowl, pour over the tomato sauce and toss to mix. Serve at once, sprinkled with more parsley.

Pasta with Cream and Parmesan

Pasta Alfredo

This popular classic originated in Rome. It is incredibly quick and simple to make, perfect for a decadent lunch or hurried midweek supper.

Ingredients
350 g/12 oz dried fettuccine
25 g/1 oz/2 tbsp butter
300 ml/½ pint/1¼ cups double (heavy) cream
50 g/2 oz/⅔ cup grated Parmesan cheese, plus extra to serve
30 ml/2 tbsp finely chopped fresh flat leaf parsley, plus extra to garnish
salt and freshly ground black pepper
serves 3–4

Variation
In Rome, fettuccine would traditionally be served with this sauce, but tagliatelle can be used if you prefer. Pasta shapes, such as penne, rigatoni or farfalle, are also suitable.

1 Cook the fettuccine in a large pan of rapidly boiling salted water for 8–10 minutes or until *al dente*.

2 ▲ Meanwhile, melt the butter in a large, heavy pan and add the cream and Parmesan, with salt and pepper to taste. Stir over a medium heat until the cheese has melted and the sauce has thickened.

3 ▲ Drain the fettuccine thoroughly and add it to the sauce with the chopped parsley. Fold the pasta and sauce together over a medium heat until the strands of pasta are generously coated. Grind more black pepper over and garnish with the extra chopped parsley. Serve at once, with a bowl of grated Parmesan handed round separately.

Tagliatelle with Bolognese Sauce

Tagliatelle alla bolognese

Most people think of bolognese sauce, the famous ragù from Bologna, as being served with spaghetti. To be absolutely correct, it should be served with tagliatelle.

Ingredients

30 ml/2 tbsp olive oil
1 onion, finely chopped
1 carrot, finely chopped
1 celery stick, finely chopped
1 garlic clove, crushed
350 g/12 oz minced (ground) beef
150 ml/1/4 pint/2/3 cup red wine
250 ml/8 fl oz/1 cup milk
400 g/14 oz can chopped tomatoes
15 ml/1 tbsp sun-dried tomato paste
350 g/12 oz dried tagliatelle
salt and freshly ground black pepper
shredded fresh basil, to garnish
grated Parmesan cheese, to serve
serves 4

1 ▲ Heat the oil in a large, heavy pan. Add the onion, carrot, celery and garlic and cook gently, stirring frequently, for about 10 minutes until softened. Do not allow the vegetables to colour.

2 ▲ Add the minced beef to the pan with the vegetables and cook over a medium heat until the meat changes colour, stirring constantly and breaking up any lumps with a wooden spoon.

3 ▲ Pour in the wine. Stir frequently until it has evaporated, then add the milk and continue cooking and stirring until this has evaporated, too.

Cook's Tip

Don't skimp on the cooking time – it is essential for a full-flavoured bolognese sauce. Some Italian cooks insist on cooking it for 3–4 hours, so the longer the better.

4 ▲ Stir in the tomatoes and tomato paste, with salt and pepper to taste. Simmer the sauce uncovered, over the lowest possible heat for at least 45 minutes.

5 Cook the tagliatelle in a large pan of rapidly boiling salted water for 8–10 minutes or until *al dente*. Drain thoroughly and tip into a warmed large bowl. Pour over the sauce and toss to combine. Garnish with basil and serve at once, with Parmesan cheese handed separately.

Penne with Pancetta and Cream

Penne alla carbonara

This makes a gloriously rich supper dish. Follow it with a simple salad.

Ingredients
300 g/11 oz dried penne
30 ml/2 tbsp olive oil
1 small onion, finely chopped
175 g/6 oz pancetta rashers, any rinds removed, cut into bite-size strips
1–2 garlic cloves, crushed
5 egg yolks
175 ml/6 fl oz/¾ cup double (heavy) cream
115 g/4 oz/1⅓ cups grated Parmesan cheese, plus extra to serve
salt and freshly ground black pepper
serves 3–4

1 ▲ Cook the penne in a large pan of rapidly boiling salted water for about 10 minutes or until *al dente*.

2 Meanwhile, heat the oil in a large, heavy pan. Add the onion and cook gently for about 5 minutes, stirring frequently, until softened. Add the pancetta and garlic. Cook over a medium heat until the pancetta is cooked but not crisp. Remove the pan from the heat and set aside.

3 ▲ Put the egg yolks in a jug and add the cream and Parmesan cheese. Grind in plenty of black pepper. Beat well to mix.

4 ▲ Drain the penne thoroughly, tip into the pan and toss over a medium to high heat until the pancetta mixture is evenly mixed with the pasta.

5 Remove from the heat, pour in the egg yolk mixture and toss well to combine. Spoon into a large shallow serving dish, grind a little black pepper over and sprinkle with some of the extra Parmesan. Serve the rest of the Parmesan separately.

Cook's Tip
Serve this dish the moment it is ready or it will not be hot enough. Having added the egg yolks, don't return the pan to the heat or attempt to reheat the pasta and sauce together or the egg yolks will scramble and give the pasta a curdled appearance.

Farfalle with Mushrooms and Cheese

Farfalle boscaiole

Fresh wild mushrooms are very good in this sauce, but they can be very expensive. To cut the cost, use half wild and half cultivated, or as many wild as you can afford – even a small handful will intensify the mushroom flavour.

Ingredients

15 g/½ oz/1 cup dried porcini mushrooms
25 g/1 oz/2 tbsp butter
1 small onion, finely chopped
1 garlic clove, crushed
225 g/8 oz/3 cups fresh mushrooms, thinly sliced
a few fresh sage leaves, very finely chopped, plus a few whole leaves, to garnish
150 ml/¼ pint/⅔ cup dry white wine
225 g/8 oz/2 cups dried farfalle
115 g/4 oz/½ cup mascarpone cheese
115 g/4 oz/1 cup Gorgonzola or torta di Gorgonzola cheese, crumbled
salt and freshly ground black pepper
serves 4

1 ▲ Put the dried porcini in a small bowl with 250 ml/8 fl oz/1 cup warm water and leave to soak for 20–30 minutes. Remove from the liquid and squeeze the porcini over the bowl to extract as much liquid as possible. Strain the liquid and set it aside. Finely chop the porcini.

2 Melt the butter in a large saucepan, add the onion and chopped porcini and cook gently, stirring for about 3 minutes until the onion is soft. Add the garlic and fresh mushrooms, chopped sage, salt and plenty of black pepper. Cook over a medium heat, stirring frequently, for about 5 minutes or until the mushrooms are soft and juicy. Stir in the soaking liquid and the wine and simmer.

3 ▲ Cook the farfalle in a large saucepan of rapidly boiling salted water, for about 10 minutes or until *al dente*.

Variation

For a lighter sauce, use crème fraîche instead of mascarpone.

4 ▲ Meanwhile, stir the mascarpone and Gorgonzola into the mushroom sauce. Heat through, stirring, until melted. Taste for seasoning. Drain the pasta thoroughly, add to the sauce and toss to mix. Serve at once, with black pepper ground liberally on top. Garnish with sage leaves.

Pasta with Tomato and Chilli Sauce

Pasta all'arrabbiata

This is a speciality of Lazio – the word arrabbiata means rabid or angry, and describes the heat that comes from the chilli. This quick version is made with bottled sugocasa.

Ingredients

500 g/1 lb sugocasa (see Cook's Tip)
2 garlic cloves, crushed
150 ml/¼ pint/⅔ cup dry white wine
15 ml/1 tbsp sun-dried tomato paste
1 fresh red chilli
300 g/11 oz penne or tortiglioni
60 ml/4 tbsp finely chopped fresh flat leaf parsley
salt and freshly ground black pepper
freshly grated Pecorino cheese, to serve

serves 4

1 ▲ Put the sugocasa, garlic, wine, tomato paste and whole chilli in a large pan and bring to the boil. Cover and simmer gently.

2 ▲ Drop the pasta into a large pan of rapidly boiling salted water and simmer for 10–12 minutes or until the pasta is *al dente*.

Cook's Tip

Sugocasa is sold in bottles sometimes labelled "crushed Italian tomatoes". It is finer than canned chopped tomatoes and coarser than passata, so is ideal for making pasta sauces, soups and stews.

3 ▲ Remove the chilli from the sauce and add half the parsley. Taste for seasoning. If you prefer a hotter taste, chop some or all of the chilli and return it to the sauce.

4 ▲ Drain the pasta and tip into a warmed large bowl. Pour the sauce over the pasta and toss to mix. Serve at once, sprinkled with grated Pecorino and the remaining parsley.

Three-cheese Lasagne

Lasagne ai tre formaggi

The cheese makes this lasagne quite expensive, so reserve it for a special occasion.

Ingredients
30 ml/2 tbsp olive oil
1 onion, finely chopped
1 carrot, finely chopped
1 celery stick, finely chopped
1 garlic clove, crushed
675 g/1½ lb minced (ground) beef
400 g/14 oz can chopped tomatoes
300 ml/½ pint/1¼ cups beef stock
300 ml/½ pint/1¼ cups red wine
30 ml/2 tbsp sun-dried tomato paste
10 ml/2 tsp dried oregano
9 sheets no-precook lasagne
3 x 150 g/5 oz packets mozzarella cheese, thinly sliced
450 g/1 lb/2 cups ricotta cheese
115 g/4 oz Parmesan cheese, grated
salt and freshly ground black pepper
serves 6–8

1 Heat the oil and gently cook the onion, carrot, celery and garlic, stirring for 10 minutes until softened.

2 Add the beef and cook until it changes colour, stirring constantly and breaking up the meat.

3 ▲ Add the tomatoes, stock, wine, tomato paste, oregano and salt and pepper and bring to the boil, stirring. Cover, lower the heat and simmer gently for 1 hour, stirring occasionally.

4 ▲ Preheat the oven to 190°C/375°F/Gas 5. Check for seasoning, then ladle one-third of the meat sauce into a 23 x 33 cm/9 x 13 in baking dish and cover with 3 sheets of lasagne. Arrange one-third of the mozzarella slices over the top, dot with one-third of the ricotta, then sprinkle with one-third of the Parmesan.

5 Repeat these layers twice, then bake for 40 minutes. Leave to cool for 10 minutes before serving.

Tortiglioni with Spicy Sausage Sauce

Tortiglioni alla siciliana

This heady pasta dish is not for the faint-hearted. Serve it with a robust Sicilian red wine.

Ingredients
30 ml/2 tbsp olive oil
1 onion, finely chopped
1 celery stick, finely chopped
2 large garlic cloves, crushed
1 fresh red chilli, seeded and chopped
450 g/1 lb ripe Italian plum tomatoes, peeled and finely chopped
30 ml/2 tbsp tomato paste
150 ml/¼ pint/⅔ cup red wine
5 ml/1 tsp sugar
300 g/11 oz dried tortiglioni
175 g/6 oz spicy salami, rind removed
salt and freshly ground black pepper
30 ml/2 tbsp chopped fresh parsley, to garnish
grated Parmesan cheese, to serve
serves 4

Cook's Tip
Buy the salami for this dish in one piece so that you can chop it into large chunks.

1 ▲ Heat the oil, then add the onion, celery, garlic and chilli and cook gently, stirring frequently, for about 10 minutes until softened.

2 Add the tomatoes, tomato purée, wine, sugar and salt and pepper to taste and bring to the boil, stirring. Lower the heat, cover and simmer gently, stirring occasionally, for about 20 minutes. Add a few spoonfuls of water from time to time if the sauce becomes too thick.

3 ▲ Meanwhile, drop the pasta into a large saucepan of rapidly boiling salted water and simmer, uncovered, for 10–12 minutes.

4 Chop the salami into bite-size chunks and add to the sauce. Heat through, then taste for seasoning.

5 Drain the pasta, tip it into a large bowl, then pour the sauce over and toss to mix. Scatter over the parsley and serve with grated Parmesan.

Spinach and Ricotta Gnocchi

Gnocchi de spinaci e ricotta

The mixture for these tasty little herb dumplings needs to be handled very carefully to achieve light and fluffy results. Serve with a sage butter and grated Parmesan.

Ingredients

6 garlic cloves, unpeeled
25 g/1 oz mixed fresh herbs, such as parsley, basil, thyme, coriander (cilantro) and chives, finely chopped
225 g/8 oz fresh spinach leaves
250 g/9 oz/generous 1 cup ricotta cheese
1 egg yolk
50 g/2 oz/$^{2}/_{3}$ cup grated Parmesan cheese
75 g/3 oz/$^{2}/_{3}$ cup plain (all-purpose) flour
50 g/2 oz/$^{1}/_{4}$ cup butter
30 ml/2 tbsp fresh sage, chopped
salt and freshly ground black pepper
serves 4

1 Cook the garlic cloves in boiling water for 4 minutes. Drain and pop out of the skins. Place in a food processor with the herbs and blend to a purée or mash the garlic with a fork and add the herbs to mix well.

2 ▲ Place the spinach in a large pan with just the water that clings to the leaves and cook gently until wilted. Leave to cool then squeeze out as much liquid as possible. Chop finely.

3 Place the ricotta in a bowl and beat in the egg yolk, spinach, herbs and garlic. Stir in half the Parmesan, sift in the flour and mix well.

Cook's Tip

Squeeze the spinach dry to ensure the gnocchi are not wet and to give a lighter result. The mixture should be fairly soft and will be easier to handle if chilled for an hour before preparing the dumplings.

4 ▲ Using lightly floured hands, break off pieces of the mixture slightly smaller than a walnut and roll into small dumplings.

5 Bring a large pan of salted water to the boil and carefully add the gnocchi. When they rise to the top of the pan they are cooked; this should take about 3 minutes.

6 ▲ The gnocchi should be light and fluffy all the way through. If not, simmer for a further minute. Drain well. Meanwhile, melt the butter in a frying pan and add the sage. Simmer gently for 1 minute. Add the gnocchi to the frying pan and toss in the butter over a gentle heat for 1 minute, then serve sprinkled with the remaining Parmesan.

Gnocchi with Gorgonzola Sauce

Gnocchi alla gorgonzola

Gnocchi are prepared all over Italy with different ingredients used in different regions. The most common are* gnocchi di patate, *potato dumplings.

Ingredients
450 g/1 lb potatoes, unpeeled
1 large (US extra large) egg
115 g/4 oz/1 cup plain (all-purpose) flour
fresh thyme sprigs, to garnish
salt and freshly ground black pepper

For the sauce
115 g/4 oz Gorgonzola cheese
60 ml/4 tbsp double (heavy) cream
15 ml/1 tbsp fresh thyme, chopped
60 ml/4 tbsp freshly grated Parmesan cheese, to serve
serves 4

1 Cook the potatoes in boiling salted water for about 20 minutes until they are tender. Drain and, when cool enough to handle, remove the skins.

2 ▲ Force the potatoes through a sieve (strainer), pressing through using the back of a spoon, into a mixing bowl. Add plenty of seasoning and then beat in the egg until completely incorporated. Add the flour a little at a time, stirring well with a wooden spoon after each addition until you have a smooth dough. (You may not need all the flour.)

3 Turn the dough out on to a floured surface and knead for about 3 minutes, adding more flour if necessary, until it is smooth and soft and not sticky to the touch.

Cook's Tip
Choose dry, floury potatoes. Avoid new or red-skinned potatoes which do not have the right dry texture.

4 ▲ Divide the dough into 6 equal pieces. Flour your hands and gently roll each piece between your hands into a log shape measuring 15–20 cm/6–8 in long and 2.5 cm/1 in around. Cut each log into 6–8 pieces, about 2.5 cm/1 in long, then gently roll each piece in the flour. Form into gnocchi by gently pressing each piece on to the floured surface with the tines of a fork to leave ridges in the dough.

5 ▲ To cook, drop the gnocchi into a pan of boiling water about 12 at a time. Once they rise to the surface, after about 2 minutes, cook for 4–5 minutes more. Remove and drain.

6 Place the Gorgonzola, cream and thyme in a large frying pan and heat gently until the cheese melts to form a thick, creamy consistency and heat through. Add the drained gnocchi and toss well to combine. Serve with Parmesan and garnish with thyme.

Rice, Polenta and Pizzas

In the north of Italy, rice is served as a first course, as creamy risotto, but you can serve it as a main dish, with a salad and Italian bread. Polenta, also from the north of Italy, is most often served with the main course, especially with meaty casseroles. Pizzas come from the south, where they are eaten at any time of day, the ultimate convenience food.

Risotto with Spring Vegetables

Risotto primavera

This is one of the prettiest risottos, especially if you can get yellow courgettes.

Ingredients

150 g/5 oz/1 cup shelled fresh peas
115 g/4 oz/1 cup green beans, cut into short lengths
30 ml/2 tbsp olive oil
75 g/3 oz/6 tbsp butter
2 small yellow courgettes (zucchini), cut into matchsticks
1 onion, finely chopped
275 g/10 oz/1½ cups risotto rice
120 ml/4 fl oz/½ cup Italian dry white vermouth
about 1 litre/1¾ pints/4 cups boiling chicken stock
75 g/3 oz/1 cup grated Parmesan cheese
a small handful of fresh basil leaves, finely shredded, plus a few whole leaves, to garnish
salt and freshly ground black pepper

serves 4

1 Blanch the peas and beans in a large pan of lightly salted boiling water for 2–3 minutes until just tender. Drain, refresh under cold running water, drain again and set aside for later.

2 ▲ Heat the oil and 25 g/1 oz/2 tbsp of the butter in a medium pan until foaming. Add the courgettes and cook gently for 2–3 minutes or until just softened. Remove with a slotted spoon and set aside. Add the onion to the pan and cook gently for about 3 minutes, stirring frequently, until it is softened.

Cook's Tip

To ensure that the rice cooks evenly only add a couple of ladlefuls of stock at a time. Wait until the stock has been almost completely absorbed by the rice before adding more.

3 ▲ Stir in the rice until the grains start to swell and burst, then add the vermouth. Stir until the vermouth stops sizzling and most of it has been absorbed by the rice, then add a few ladlefuls of the stock, with salt and pepper to taste. Stir over low heat until the stock has been absorbed.

4 Continue cooking and stirring for 20–25 minutes, adding the remaining stock a few ladlefuls at a time. The rice should be *al dente* and the risotto should have a moist and creamy appearance.

5 ▲ Gently stir in the vegetables, the remaining butter and about half the grated Parmesan. Heat through, then stir in the shredded basil and taste for seasoning. Garnish with a few whole basil leaves and serve hot, with the remaining grated Parmesan handed separately.

Variations

Shelled broad (fava) beans can be used instead of the peas and asparagus tips instead of the green beans. Use green courgettes if yellow ones are unavailable.

Rice with Peas, Ham and Cheese

Risi e bisi

A classic risotto from the Veneto. Although it is traditionally served as a first course in Italy, risi e bisi makes an excellent supper dish with hot crusty bread.

Ingredients
75 g/3 oz/6 tbsp butter
1 small onion, finely chopped
about 1 litre/1¾ pints/4 cups boiling chicken stock
275 g/10 oz/1½ cups risotto rice
150 ml/¼ pint/⅔ cup dry white wine
225 g/8 oz/2 cups frozen petits pois (baby peas), thawed
115 g/4 oz cooked ham, diced
salt and freshly ground black pepper
50 g/2 oz/⅔ cup Parmesan cheese, to serve
serves 4

1 ▲ Melt 50 g/2 oz/4 tbsp of the butter in a large, heavy pan until foaming. Add the onion and cook gently for about 3 minutes, stirring frequently, until softened. Have the hot stock ready in an adjacent pan.

2 ▲ Add the rice to the onion mixture. Stir until the grains start to burst, then pour in the wine. Stir until it stops sizzling and most of it has been absorbed, then pour in a little hot stock, with salt and pepper to taste. Stir over a low heat until the stock has been absorbed.

3 ▲ Add the remaining stock, a little at a time, allowing the rice to absorb all the liquid before adding more, and stirring constantly. Add the peas towards the end. After 20–25 minutes, the rice should be *al dente* and the risotto moist and creamy.

4 ▲ Gently stir in the diced cooked ham and the remaining butter. Heat through until the butter has melted, then taste for seasoning. Transfer to a warmed serving bowl. Grate or shave a little Parmesan over the top and hand the rest separately.

Saffron Risotto

Risotto alla milanese

This classic, delicately flavoured, risotto is always served with osso buco, but makes a delicious first course or light supper dish in its own right.

Ingredients
about 1.2 litres/2 pints/5 cups beef or chicken stock
good pinch of saffron threads or 1 sachet of saffron powder
75 g/3 oz/6 tbsp butter
1 onion, finely chopped
275 g/10 oz/1½ cups risotto rice
75 g/3 oz/1 cup grated Parmesan cheese
salt and freshly ground black pepper
serves 4

1 Bring the stock to the boil in a pan, then reduce to a low simmer. Ladle a little stock into a small bowl. Add the saffron threads or powder and leave aside to infuse (steep).

2 Melt 50 g/2 oz/4 tbsp of the butter in a large saucepan until foaming. Add the onion and cook gently for about 3 minutes, stirring frequently, until softened.

3 Add the rice. Stir until the grains start to swell and burst, then add a few ladlefuls of the stock, with the saffron liquid and salt and pepper to taste. Stir over a low heat until the stock is absorbed. Add the remaining stock, a few ladlefuls at a time, allowing the rice to absorb all the liquid before adding more, and stirring constantly. After 20–25 minutes, the rice should be *al dente* and the risotto golden yellow, moist and creamy.

4 ▲ Gently stir in about two-thirds of the grated Parmesan and the remaining butter. Heat through until the butter has melted, then taste for seasoning. Transfer the risotto to a warmed serving bowl or platter and serve hot, with the remaining grated Parmesan sprinkled on top.

Polenta Elisa

Polenta Elisa

This dish comes from the valley around Lake Como. Serve it solo as a first course, or with a mixed salad and some sliced salami or prosciutto for a midweek supper.

Ingredients
250 ml/8 fl oz/1 cup milk
225 g/8 oz/2 cups pre-cooked polenta
115 g/4 oz/1 cup grated Gruyère cheese
115 g/4 oz/1 cup torta di Dolcelatte cheese, crumbled
50 g/2 oz/¼ cup butter
2 garlic cloves, roughly chopped
a few fresh sage leaves, chopped
salt and freshly ground black pepper
prosciutto, to serve
serves 4

1 Preheat the oven to 200°C/400°F/Gas 6. Lightly butter a 20–25 cm/8–10 in baking dish.

Cook's Tip
Pour the polenta into the boiling liquid in a continuous stream, stirring constantly with a wooden spoon or balloon whisk. If using a whisk, change to a wooden spoon once the polenta thickens.

2 ▲ Bring the milk and 750ml/1¼ pints/3 cups water to the boil in a large saucepan, add 5 ml/1 tsp salt, then tip in the polenta. Cook for about 8 minutes or according to the instructions on the packet.

3 Spoon half the polenta into the baking dish and level. Cover with half the grated Gruyère and crumbled Dolcelatte. Spoon the remaining polenta evenly over the top and sprinkle with the remaining cheeses.

4 Melt the butter in a small saucepan until foaming, add the garlic and sage and fry, stirring, until the butter turns golden brown.

5 ▲ Drizzle the butter mixture over the polenta and cheese and grind black pepper liberally over the top. Bake for 5 minutes. Serve hot, with slices of prosciutto.

Risotto with Four Cheeses

Risotto ai quattro formaggi

This is a very rich dish. Serve it for a dinner-party first course, with sparkling white wine.

Ingredients
40 g/1½ oz/3 tbsp butter
1 small onion, finely chopped
1 litre/1¾ pints/4 cups boiling chicken stock
350 g/12 oz/1¾ cups risotto rice
200 ml/7 fl oz/scant 1 cup sparkling dry white wine
50 g/2 oz/½ cup grated Gruyère cheese
50 g/2 oz/½ cup Fontina cheese, diced small
50 g/2 oz/½ cup Gorgonzola cheese, crumbled
50 g/2 oz/⅔ cup grated Parmesan cheese
salt and freshly ground black pepper
fresh flat leaf parsley, to garnish
serves 6

Cook's Tip
If you're feeling especially extravagant you could use champagne for this risotto, although asti spumante is more often used as a cheaper, but still delicious, substitute.

1 Melt the butter in a large, heavy pan until foaming. Add the onion and cook gently, stirring frequently, for about 3 minutes until softened. Have the hot stock ready in an adjacent pan.

2 ▲ Add the rice and stir until the grains start to swell and burst, then add the sparkling wine. Stir until it stops sizzling and most of it has been absorbed by the rice, then pour in a little of the hot stock. Add salt and pepper to taste. Stir over a low heat until the stock has been absorbed.

3 Add more stock, a little at a time, allowing the rice to absorb it before adding more, and stirring constantly. After 20–25 minutes the rice will be *al dente* and the risotto creamy.

4 ▲ Turn off the heat under the pan, then add the Gruyère, Fontina, Gorgonzola and 30 ml/2 tbsp of the Parmesan. Stir gently until the cheeses have melted, then taste for seasoning. Tip into a serving bowl and garnish with parsley. Serve the remaining Parmesan separately.

Polenta with Mushroom Sauce

Polenta con salsa di funghi

Polenta, made from maize flour, fulfils the same function as rice, bread or potatoes in forming the starchy base for a meal. Here, it is cooked until it forms a soft dough, then flavoured with Parmesan. Its subtle taste works well with the rich mushroom sauce.

Ingredients

1.2 litres/2 pints/5 cups vegetable stock
350 g/12 oz/3 cups polenta
50 g/2 oz/ ⅔ cup grated Parmesan cheese
salt and freshly ground black pepper

For the sauce

15 g/½ oz/1 cup dried porcini mushrooms
15 ml/1 tbsp olive oil
50 g/2 oz/¼ cup butter
1 onion, finely chopped
1 carrot, finely chopped
1 celery stick, finely chopped
2 garlic cloves, crushed
450 g/1 lb/6 cups mixed chestnut and large flat mushrooms, roughly chopped
120 ml/4 fl oz/½ cup red wine
400 g/14 oz can chopped tomatoes
5 ml/1 tsp tomato purée
15 ml/1 tbsp chopped fresh thyme leaves

serves 4

1 ▲ Make the sauce. Put the dried mushrooms in a bowl, add 150 ml/¼ pint/⅔ cup of hot water and soak for 20 minutes. Drain the mushrooms, reserving the liquid, and chop roughly.

2 Heat the oil and butter in a saucepan and add the onion, carrot, celery and garlic. Cook over a low heat for about 5 minutes until the vegetables are beginning to soften, then raise the heat and add the fresh and soaked dried mushrooms to the pan of vegetables. Cook for 8 - 10 minutes until the mushrooms are softened and golden.

3 ▲ Pour in the wine and cook rapidly for 2-3 minutes until reduced, then tip in the tomatoes and reserved mushroom liquid. Stir in the tomato purée with the thyme and plenty of salt and pepper. Lower the heat and simmer for 20 minutes until the sauce is rich and thick.

Cook's Tip

The polenta will spit during cooking, so use a long-handled spoon and wrap a towel around your hand to protect it while stirring.

4 ▲ Meanwhile, heat the stock in a large, heavy pan. Add a generous pinch of salt. As soon as it simmers, tip in the polenta in a fine stream, whisking until the mixture is smooth. Cook for 30 minutes, stirring constantly, until the polenta comes away from the pan. Remove from the heat and stir in half the Parmesan and some black pepper.

5 Divide equally among four heated bowls and top each with sauce. Sprinkle with the remaining Parmesan and serve.

Ricotta and Fontina Pizza

Pizza con ricotta e fontina

The earthy mixed mushrooms' flavours are delicious with the creamy cheeses.

Ingredients

For the pizza dough

2.5 ml/½ tsp active dried yeast
pinch of sugar
450 g/1 lb/4 cups strong white bread flour
5 ml/1 tsp salt
30 ml/2 tbsp olive oil

For the tomato sauce

400 g/14 oz can chopped tomatoes
150 ml/¼ pint/⅔ cup passata (bottled strained tomatoes
1 large garlic clove, finely chopped
5 ml/1 tsp dried oregano
1 bay leaf
10 ml/2 tsp malt vinegar
salt and freshly ground black pepper

For the topping

30 ml/2 tbsp olive oil
1 garlic clove, finely chopped
350 g/12 oz/4 cups mixed mushrooms, sliced
30 ml/2 tbsp chopped fresh oregano, plus whole leaves, to garnish
250 g/9 oz/generous 1 cup ricotta cheese
225 g/8 oz Fontina cheese, sliced

makes 4 x 25 cm/10 in thin crust pizzas

1 ▲ Make the dough. Put 300 ml/½ pint/1¼ cups warm water in a measuring jug (cup). Add the yeast and sugar and leave for 5–10 minutes until frothy. Sift the flour and salt into a large bowl and make a well in the centre. Gradually pour in the yeast mixture and the olive oil. Mix to make a smooth dough. Knead on a floured surface for about 10 minutes until smooth, springy and elastic. Place the dough in a floured bowl, cover and leave to rise in a warm place for 1½ hours.

2 Meanwhile, make the tomato sauce. Place all the ingredients in a large, heavy pan, cover and bring to the boil. Lower the heat, remove the lid and simmer for 20 minutes, stirring occasionally, until reduced.

3 ▲ Make the topping. Heat the oil in a frying pan. Add the garlic and mushrooms, with salt and pepper to taste. Cook, stirring, for about 5 minutes or until the mushrooms are tender and golden. Set aside.

4 ▲ Preheat the oven to 220°C/425°F/Gas 7. Brush four baking sheets with oil. Knead the dough for 2 minutes, then divide into four equal pieces. Roll out each piece to a 25 cm/10 in round and place on a baking sheet.

5 Spoon the tomato sauce over each dough round. Brush the edge with a little olive oil. Add the mushrooms, oregano and cheese. Bake for about 15 minutes until golden brown and crisp. Scatter the oregano leaves over.

Butternut Squash and Sage Pizza

Pizza con zucca e salvia

The combination of the sweet butternut squash, sage and sharp goat's cheese works wonderfully on this pizza. Pumpkin and winter squashes are popular in northern Italy.

Ingredients

15 g/½ oz/1 tbsp butter
30 ml/2 tbsp olive oil
2 shallots, finely chopped
1 butternut squash, peeled, seeded and cubed, about 450 g/1 lb prepared weight
16 sage leaves
1 quantity risen pizza dough (see page 62)
1 quantity tomato sauce (see page 62)
115 g/4 oz/1 cup mozzarella cheese, sliced
115 g/4 oz/½ cup firm goat's cheese
salt and freshly ground black pepper

serves 4

1 ▲ Preheat the oven to 200°C/400°F/Gas 6. Oil four baking sheets. Put the butter and oil in a roasting pan and heat in the oven for a few minutes. Add the shallots, squash and half the sage leaves. Toss to coat. Roast for 15–20 minutes until tender.

2 ▲ Raise the oven temperature to 220°C/425°F/Gas 7. Divide the pizza dough into four equal pieces and roll out each piece on a lightly floured surface to a 25 cm/10 in round.

3 ▲ Transfer each round to a baking sheet and spread with the tomato sauce, leaving a 1 cm/½ in border all around. Spoon the squash and shallot mixture over the top.

4 ▲ Arrange the slices of mozzarella over the squash mixture and crumble the goat's cheese over. Scatter the remaining sage leaves over and season with plenty of salt and pepper. Bake for 15–20 minutes until the cheese has melted and the crust on each pizza is golden.

Fried Pizza Pasties

Panzerotti

These tasty little morsels are served all over central and southern Italy as a snack food or as part of a hot antipasti. Although similar to calzone they are fried instead of baked.

Ingredients
½ quantity pizza dough (see page 62)
½ quantity tomato sauce (see page 62)
225 g/8 oz mozzarella cheese, chopped
115 g/4 oz Italian salami, thinly sliced
handful of fresh basil leaves, roughly torn
sunflower oil, for deep frying
salt and freshly ground black pepper
serves 4

Cook's Tip
To test that the oil is ready, carefully drop a piece of bread into the oil. If it sizzles instantly, the oil is ready.

1 Preheat the oven to 200°C/400°F/ Gas 6. Brush two baking sheets with oil. Divide the dough into 12 and roll out each piece on a lightly floured surface to a 10 cm/4 in round.

2 ▲ Spread the centre of each round with a little of the tomato sauce, leaving sufficient border all round for sealing the pasty, then top with a few pieces of mozzarella and salami slices. Sprinkle with salt and freshly ground black pepper and add a few fresh basil leaves to each round.

3 ▲ Brush the edges of the dough rounds with a little water, then fold over and press together to seal.

4 Heat oil to a depth of about 10 cm/ 4 in in a heavy-based pan. When hot, deep-fry the pasties, a few at a time, for 8-10 minutes until golden. Drain on kitchen paper and serve hot.

Sicilian Pizza

Pizza alla siciliana

This robust-flavoured pizza is topped with mozzarella and Pecorino cheeses.

Ingredients
1 small aubergine (eggplant), cut into thin rounds
30 ml/2 tbsp olive oil
½ quantity risen pizza dough (see page 62)
½ quantity tomato sauce (see page 62)
175 g/6 oz mozzarella cheese, sliced
50 g/2 oz/½ cup pitted black olives
15 ml/1 tbsp drained capers
60 ml/4 tbsp grated Pecorino cheese
salt and freshly ground black pepper
serves 2

Cook's Tip
For best results choose olives that have been marinated in extra virgin olive oil and flavoured with herbs and garlic.

1 ▲ Preheat the oven to 200°C/400°F/ Gas 6. Brush one or two baking sheets with oil. Brush the aubergine rounds with olive oil and arrange them on the baking sheet(s). Bake for 10-15 minutes, turning once, until browned and tender. Remove the aubergine slices from the baking sheet(s) and drain on kitchen paper.

2 Raise the oven temperature to 220°C/425°F/Gas 7. Roll out the pizza dough to two 25 cm/10 in rounds. Transfer to baking sheets and spread with the tomato sauce.

3 ▲ Pile the aubergine slices on top of the tomato sauce and cover with the mozzarella. Dot with the black olives and capers. Sprinkle the Pecorino cheese liberally over the top, and season with plenty of salt and pepper. Bake for 15-20 minutes until the crust on each pizza is golden.

Seafood, Poultry and Meat

Italy has such an extensive coastline – and so many lakes, rivers and streams – that it is small wonder that fish and shellfish are so popular. The Italians also eat a wide variety of different meats, and tastes vary according to region. All meats are eaten as a second course – *secondo piatto* – usually simple and served solo, with vegetables to follow.

Pan-fried Prawns in their Shells

Gamberi fritti in padella

Although expensive, this is a very quick and simple dish, ideal for an impromptu supper with friends. Serve with hot crusty Italian bread to scoop up the juices.

Ingredients

60 ml/4 tbsp extra virgin olive oil
32 large fresh prawns (large shrimp), in their shells
4 garlic cloves, finely chopped
120 ml/4 fl oz/½ cup Italian dry white vermouth
45 ml/3 tbsp passata (bottle strained tomatoes)
salt and freshly ground black pepper
chopped fresh flat leaf parsley, to garnish
crusty bread, to serve
serves 4

Cook's Tip

Prawns in their shells are sweet and juicy, and fun to eat with your fingers. They can be quite messy though, so provide guests with finger bowls and napkins.

1 ▲ Heat the olive oil in a large heavy-based frying pan until just sizzling. Add the prawns and toss over a medium to high heat until their shells just begin to turn pink. Sprinkle the garlic over the prawns in the pan and toss again, then add the vermouth and let it bubble, tossing the prawns constantly so that they cook evenly and absorb the flavours of the garlic and vermouth.

2 ▲ Keeping the pan on the heat, add the passata, with salt and pepper to taste. Stir until the prawns are thoroughly coated in the sauce. Serve at once, sprinkled with the parsley and accompanied by plenty of hot crusty bread.

Grilled Red Mullet with Rosemary

Triglie al rosmarino

This recipe is very simple to make – the taste of freshly grilled red mullet is so good in itself that it needs very little to bring out the tender and juicy flavours.

Ingredients

4 red mullet, cleaned, about 275 g/10 oz each
4 garlic cloves, cut lengthways into thin slivers
75 ml/5 tbsp olive oil
30 ml/2 tbsp balsamic vinegar
10 ml/2 tsp very finely chopped fresh rosemary or 5 ml/1 tsp dried rosemary
freshly ground black pepper
coarse sea salt, to serve
fresh rosemary sprigs and lemon wedges, to garnish
serves 4

Variation

Red mullet are extra delicious cooked on the barbecue. If possible, enclose them in a basket grill so that they are easy to turn over.

1 ▲ Cut three diagonal slits in both sides of each fish. Push the garlic slivers into the slits. Place the fish in a single layer in a shallow dish. Whisk the oil, vinegar and rosemary, with ground black pepper to taste.

2 ▲ Pour over the fish, cover with clear film and leave to marinate in a cool place for about 1 hour. Put the fish on the rack of a grill (broiling) pan and grill (broil) for 5–6 minutes on each side, turning once and brushing with the marinade. Serve hot, sprinkled with coarse sea salt and garnished with fresh rosemary sprigs and lemon wedges.

Pan-fried Sole with Lemon

Sogliole al limone

The delicate flavour and texture of sole is brought out in this simple, classic recipe. Lemon sole is used here because it is easier to obtain – and less expensive – than Dover sole.

Ingredients

30–45 ml/2–3 tbsp plain (all-purpose) flour
4 lemon sole fillets
45 ml/3 tbsp olive oil
50 g/2 oz/¼ cup butter
60 ml/4 tbsp lemon juice
30 ml/2 tbsp rinsed bottled capers
salt and freshly ground black pepper
fresh flat leaf parsley and lemon wedges, to garnish

serves 2

Cook's Tip

It is important to cook the pan juices to the right colour after removing the fish. Too pale, and they will taste insipid, too dark, and they may taste bitter. Take great care not to be distracted at this point so that you can watch the colour of the juices change to a golden brown.

1 ▲ Season the flour with salt and black pepper. Coat the sole fillets evenly on both sides. Heat the oil with half the butter in a large shallow pan until foaming. Add two sole fillets and fry over a medium heat for 2–3 minutes on each side.

2 Lift out the sole fillets with a fish slice or metal spatula and place on a warmed serving platter. Keep hot. Fry the remaining sole fillets.

3 ▲ Remove the pan from the heat and add the lemon juice and remaining butter. Return the pan to a high heat and stir vigorously until the pan juices are sizzling and beginning to turn golden brown. Remove from the heat and stir in the capers.

4 Pour the pan juices over the sole, sprinkle with salt and pepper to taste and garnish with the parsley. Add the lemon wedges and serve at once.

Three-colour Fish Kebabs

Spiedini tricolore

Don't let the fish marinate for more than an hour. The lemon juice will start to break down the fibres of the fish after this time and it will be difficult not to overcook it.

Ingredients

120 ml/4 fl oz/½ cup olive oil
finely grated rind and juice of 1 large lemon
5 ml/1 tsp crushed chilli flakes
350 g/12 oz monkfish fillet, cubed
350 g/12 oz swordfish fillet, cubed
350 g/12 oz thick salmon fillet or steak, cubed
2 red, yellow or orange (bell) peppers, cored, seeded and cut into squares
30 ml/2 tbsp finely chopped fresh flat leaf parsley
salt and freshly ground black pepper

For the sweet tomato and chilli salsa

225 g/8 oz ripe tomatoes, finely chopped
1 garlic clove, crushed
1 fresh red chilli, seeded and chopped
45 ml/3 tbsp extra virgin olive oil
15 ml/1 tbsp lemon juice
15 ml/1 tbsp finely chopped fresh flat leaf parsley
pinch of sugar
serves 4

1 ▲ Put the oil in a shallow glass or china bowl and add the lemon rind and juice, the chilli flakes and pepper to taste. Whisk to combine, then add the fish chunks. Turn to coat evenly.

2 Add the pepper squares, stir, then cover and marinate in a cool place for 1 hour, turning occasionally.

Variation

Use tuna instead of swordfish. It has a similar meaty texture.

3 ▲ Thread the fish and peppers on to eight oiled metal skewers, reserving the marinade. Cook the skewered fish on a barbecue or under a grill (broiler) for 5–8 minutes, turning once.

4 Meanwhile, make the salsa by mixing all the ingredients in a bowl, and seasoning to taste with salt and pepper. Heat the reserved marinade in a small pan, remove from the heat and stir in the parsley, with salt and pepper to taste. Serve the kebabs hot, with the marinade spooned over, accompanied by the salsa.

Roast Sea Bass

Branzino al forno

Sea bass has meaty flesh. It is an expensive fish, best cooked as simply as possible. Avoid elaborate sauces, which would mask its delicate flavour.

Ingredients

1 fennel bulb with fronds, about 275 g/10 oz
2 lemons
120 ml/4 fl oz/½ cup olive oil
1 small red onion, diced
2 sea bass, about 500 g/1¼ lb each, cleaned with heads left on
120 ml/4 fl oz/½ cup dry white wine
salt and freshly ground black pepper
lemon slices, to garnish
serves 4

1 ▲ Preheat the oven to 190°C/375°F/ Gas 5. Cut the fronds off the top of the fennel and reserve for the garnish. Cut the fennel bulb lengthways into thin wedges, then into dice. Cut one half lemon into four slices. Squeeze the juice from the remaining lemon half and the other lemon.

2 ▲ Heat 30 ml/2 tbsp of the oil in a frying pan, add the diced fennel and onion and cook gently, stirring frequently, for about 5 minutes until softened. Remove from the heat.

3 ▲ Make three diagonal slashes on both sides of each sea bass with a sharp knife. Brush a roasting pan generously with oil, add the fish and tuck two lemon slices in each cavity. Scatter the softened fennel and onion over the fish.

Cook's Tip

Farmed or wild sea bass are available all year round from the fishmonger. They are expensive, but well worth buying for a special main course. Sizes vary from the ones used here, which are a very good size for two servings, to 1.5–1.75 kg/ 3–4½ lb, which take up to 50 minutes to cook.

4 ▲ Whisk the remaining oil, the lemon juice and salt and pepper to taste and pour over the fish. Cover with foil and roast for 30 minutes or until the flesh flakes, removing the foil for the last 10 minutes. Discard the lemon slices, transfer the fish to a heated serving platter and keep hot.

5 Put the roasting pan on top of the stove. Add the wine and stir over a medium heat to incorporate all the pan juices. Bring to the boil, then spoon the juices over the fish. Garnish with the reserved fennel fronds and lemon slices and serve at once.

Stuffed Swordfish Rolls

Involtini di pesce spada

This is a very tasty dish, with strong flavours from the tomato, olive and caper sauce – and from the salty Pecorino cheese. If you like, substitute Parmesan cheese, which is milder.

Ingredients

30 ml/2 tbsp olive oil
1 small onion, finely chopped
1 celery stick, finely chopped
450 g/1 lb ripe Italian plum tomatoes, chopped
115 g/4 oz pitted green olives, half roughly chopped, half left whole
45 ml/3 tbsp drained bottled capers
4 large swordfish steaks, each about 1 cm / ½ in thick and 115 g/4 oz in weight
1 egg
50 g/2 oz/⅔ cup grated Pecorino cheese
25 g/1 oz/½ cup fresh white breadcrumbs
salt and freshly ground black pepper
sprigs of fresh parsley, to garnish
serves 4

Cook's Tip

This dish is not for the inexperienced cook because the pounding, stuffing and rolling of the fish is quite tricky. If you prefer, you can omit the stuffing and simply cook the swordfish steaks in the sauce.

1 ▲ Heat the oil in a large heavy-based frying pan. Add the onion and celery and cook gently for about 3 minutes, stirring frequently. Stir in the tomatoes, olives and capers, with salt and pepper to taste. Bring to the boil, then lower the heat, cover and simmer for about 15 minutes. Stir occasionally and add a little water if the sauce becomes too thick.

2 Remove the fish skin and place each steak between two sheets of clear film (plastic wrap). Pound lightly with a rolling pin until each steak is reduced to about 5 mm/¼ in thick.

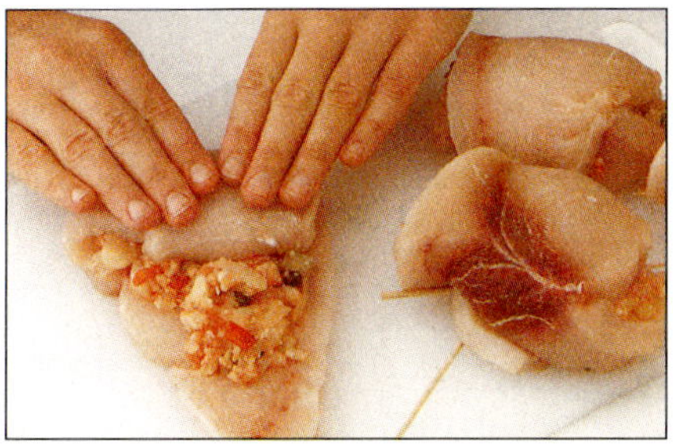

3 ▲ Beat the egg in a bowl and add the cheese, breadcrumbs and a few spoonfuls of the sauce. Stir well to mix to a moist stuffing. Spread one-quarter of the stuffing over each swordfish steak, then roll up into a sausage shape. Secure with wooden cocktail sticks (toothpicks).

4 ▲ Add the rolls to the sauce in the pan and bring to the boil. Lower the heat, cover and simmer for about 30 minutes, turning once. Add a little water as the sauce reduces.

5 Remove the rolls from the sauce and discard the cocktail sticks. Place on warmed dinner plates and spoon the sauce over and around. Garnish with the parsley and serve hot.

Chicken with Parma Ham and Cheese

Pollo alla valdostana

The name Valdostana is derived from Val d'Aosta, home of the Fontina cheese used here.

Ingredients

2 thin slices of prosciutto
2 thin slices of Fontina cheese
4 part-boned chicken breasts
4 sprigs of basil
30 ml/2 tbsp olive oil
15 g/½ oz/1 tbsp butter
120 ml/4 fl oz/½ cup dry white wine
salt and freshly ground black pepper
tender young salad leaves, to serve
serves 4

Cook's Tip

There is nothing quite like the buttery texture and nutty flavour of Fontina cheese, and it also has superb melting qualities, but you could use a Swiss or French mountain cheese, such as Gruyère or Emmental. Ask for the cheese to be sliced thinly on the machine slicer, as you will find it difficult to slice it thinly yourself.

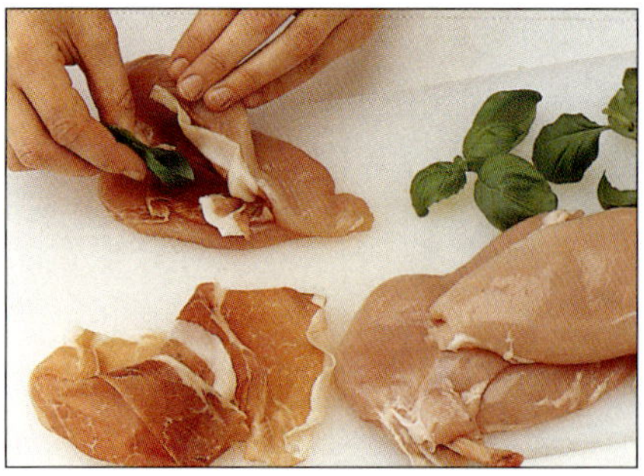

1 ▲ Preheat the oven to 200°C/400°F/Gas 6. Lightly oil a baking dish. Cut the prosciutto and Fontina slices in half crossways. Skin the chicken breasts, open out the slit in the centre of each one, and fill each cavity with half a ham slice and a basil sprig.

2 ▲ Heat the oil and butter in a wide heavy-based frying pan until foaming. Cook the chicken over a medium heat for 2 minutes on each side until golden. Transfer to the baking dish.

3 ▲ Add the white wine to the remaining juices in the pan the chicken was cooked in. Stir over a medium heat until the juices are combined and sizzling, then pour over the chicken and season with salt and pepper to taste.

4 Top each chicken breast with a slice of Fontina. Bake for about 20 minutes or until the chicken is tender. Serve hot, with tender young salad leaves or seasonal vegetables.

Devilled Chicken

Pollo alla diavola

You can tell this spicy, grilled chicken dish comes from southern Italy because it has dried red chillies in the marinade. Versions without the chillies are just as good.

Ingredients

120 ml/4 fl oz/½ cup olive oil
finely grated rind and juice of 1 large lemon
2 garlic cloves, finely chopped
10 ml/2 tsp finely chopped or crumbled dried red chillies
12 skinless, boneless chicken thighs, each cut into 3 or 4 pieces
salt and freshly ground black pepper
flat leaf parsley leaves, to garnish
lemon wedges, to serve
serves 4

Cook's Tip

Thread the chicken pieces spiral-fashion on the skewers so they do not fall off during cooking.

1 ▲ Make a marinade by mixing the oil, lemon rind and juice, garlic and chillies in a large, shallow glass or china dish. Add salt and pepper to taste. Whisk well, then add the chicken pieces, turning to coat with the marinade. Cover and marinate in the refrigerator for at least 4 hours, or preferably overnight.

2 ▲ When ready to cook, prepare the barbecue or preheat the grill (broiler) and thread the chicken pieces on to eight oiled metal skewers. Cook on the barbecue or under a hot grill for 6–8 minutes, turning frequently, until tender. Garnish with parsley leaves and serve hot, with lemon wedges for squeezing.

Turkey with Marsala Cream Sauce

Tacchino al marsala

Marsala makes a very rich and tasty sauce. The addition of lemon juice gives it a sharp edge, which helps to offset the richness of the cream.

Ingredients

6 turkey breast steaks
45 ml/3 tbsp plain (all-purpose) flour
30 ml/2 tbsp olive oil
25 g/1 oz/2 tbsp butter
175 ml/6 fl oz/¾ cup dry Marsala
60 ml/4 tbsp lemon juice
175 ml/6 fl oz/¾ cup double (heavy) cream
salt and freshly ground black pepper
lemon wedges, and chopped fresh parsley
mangetouts (snow peas) and green beans, to serve

serves 6

1 ▲ Put each turkey steak between two sheets of clear film (plastic wrap) and pound with a rolling pin to flatten and stretch. Cut each steak in half or into quarters, cutting away and discarding any sinew.

2 ▲ Spread out the flour in a shallow bowl. Season well and coat the meat.

Variation

Veal or pork escalopes (US scallops) or chicken breast fillets can be used instead of the turkey, and 50 g/2 oz/¼ cup mascarpone cheese instead of the double cream.

3 ▲ Heat the oil and butter in a wide heavy-based saucepan or frying pan until sizzling. Add as many pieces of turkey as the pan will hold and sauté over a medium heat for about 3 minutes on each side until crispy and tender. Transfer to a warmed serving dish with tongs and keep hot. Repeat with the remaining turkey.

4 ▲ Lower the heat. Mix the Marsala and lemon juice in a jug, add to the pan and raise the heat. Bring to the boil, stirring in the sediment, then add the cream. Simmer, stirring constantly, until the sauce is reduced and glossy. Taste for seasoning. Spoon over the turkey, garnish with the lemon wedges and parsley and serve at once with the mangetouts and green beans.

Pork in Sweet and Sour Sauce

Scaloppine di maiale in agrodolce

The combination of sweet and sour flavours is popular in Venetian cooking, especially with meat and liver. This recipe is given extra bite with the addition of crushed mixed peppercorns. Served with shelled broad beans tossed with grilled bacon – it is delectable.

Ingredients

1 whole pork fillet, about 350 g/12 oz
25 ml/1½ tbsp plain (all-purpose) flour
30–45 ml/2–3 tbsp olive oil
250 ml/8 fl oz/1 cup dry white wine
30 ml/2 tbsp white wine vinegar
10 ml/2 tsp sugar
15 ml/1 tbsp mixed peppercorns, coarsely ground
salt and freshly ground black pepper
broad (fava) beans tossed with grilled bacon, to serve

serves 2

1 ▲ Cut the pork diagonally into thin slices. Place between two sheets of clear film (plastic wrap) and pound lightly with a rolling pin to flatten them evenly.

2 ▲ Spread out the flour in a shallow bowl. Season well and coat the meat.

Cook's Tip

Grind the peppercorns in a pepper grinder, or crush them with a mortar and pestle.

3 ▲ Heat 15 ml/1 tbsp of the oil in a wide heavy-based pan and add as many slices of pork as the pan will hold. Fry over a medium to high heat for 2–3 minutes on each side until crispy and tender. Remove with a fish slice or metal spatula and set aside. Repeat with the remaining pork, adding more oil as necessary.

4 ▲ Mix the wine, wine vinegar and sugar in a jug (pitcher). Pour into the pan and stir vigorously over a high heat until reduced, scraping the pan to incorporate the sediment. Stir in the peppercorns and return the pork to the pan. Spoon the sauce over the pork until it is evenly coated and heated through.

Roast Lamb with Rosemary

Agnello al rosmarino

In Italy, lamb is traditionally served at Easter. This simple roast with potatoes owes its wonderful flavour to the aromas of fresh rosemary and garlic. It makes the perfect Sunday lunch at any time of year, and is best served with one or two lightly cooked fresh vegetables, such as potatoes, broccoli, spinach or baby carrots.

Ingredients

½ leg of lamb, about 1.4 kg/3 lb
2 garlic cloves, cut lengthways into thin slivers
leaves from 4 sprigs of fresh rosemary, finely chopped
105 ml/7 tbsp olive oil
about 250 ml/8 fl oz/1 cup lamb or vegetable stock
675 g/1½ lb potatoes, cut into 2.5 cm/1 in cubes
a few fresh sage leaves, chopped
salt and freshly ground black pepper
lightly cooked baby carrots, to serve

serves 4

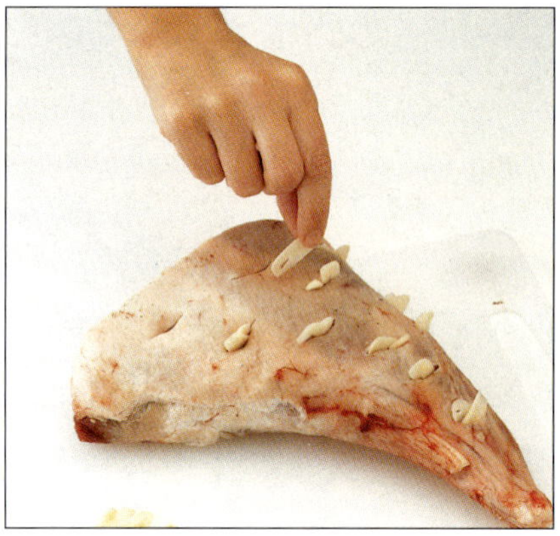

1 ▲ Preheat the oven to 230°C/450°F/Gas 8. Using the point of a sharp knife, make deep incisions in the lamb, especially near the bone, and insert the slivers of garlic.

2 ▲ Put the lamb in a roasting pan and rub it all over with 45 ml/3 tbsp of the oil. Sprinkle over about half of the chopped rosemary, patting it on firmly, and season with plenty of salt and pepper. Roast for 30 minutes, turning once.

3 ▲ Lower the oven temperature to 190°C/375°F/Gas 5. Turn the lamb over again and add 120 ml/4 fl oz/½ cup of the stock.

4 Roast for a further 1¼ -1½ hours until the lamb is tender, turning the joint two or three times more and adding the rest of the stock in two or three batches. Baste the lamb each time it is turned.

5 ▲ Meanwhile, put the potatoes in a separate roasting pan and toss with the remaining oil and rosemary and the sage. Roast, on the same oven shelf if possible, for 45 minutes, turning the potatoes several times until they are golden and tender.

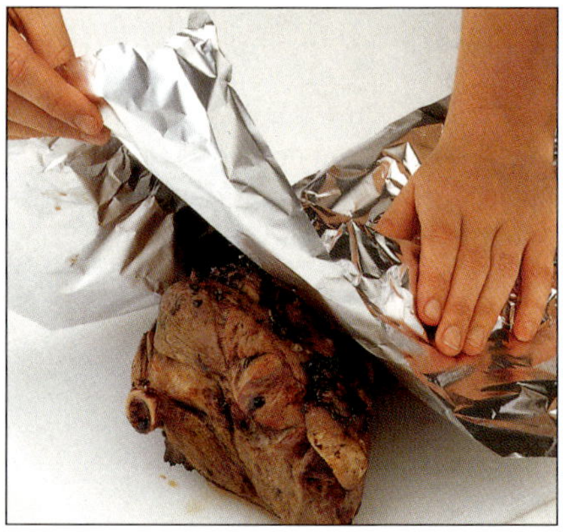

6 ▲ Transfer the lamb to a carving board, tent with foil and leave in a warm place for 10 minutes so that the flesh firms for easier carving. Serve whole or carved into thin slices, surrounded by the potatoes and accompanied by baby carrots.

Cook's Tip

If you like, the cooking juices can be strained and used to make a thin gravy with stock and red wine.

Veal Shanks with Tomatoes and White Wine

Osso buco

This famous Milanese dish is rich and hearty. It is traditionally served with risotto alla milanese, but plain boiled rice goes equally well. The lemony gremolata garnish helps to cut the richness of the dish, as does a crisp green salad – serve it after the osso buco and before the dessert, to refresh the palate.

Ingredients

30 ml/2 tbsp plain (all-purpose) flour
4 pieces of osso buco
2 small onions
30 ml/2 tbsp olive oil
1 large celery stick, finely chopped
1 medium carrot, finely chopped
2 garlic cloves, finely chopped
400 g/14 oz can chopped tomatoes
300 ml/½ pint/1¼ cups dry white wine
300 ml/½ pint/1¼ cups chicken or veal stock
1 strip of thinly pared lemon rind
2 bay leaves, plus extra for garnishing (optional)
salt and freshly ground black pepper

For the gremolata

30 ml/2 tbsp finely chopped fresh flat leaf parsley
finely grated rind of 1 lemon
1 garlic clove, finely chopped

serves 4

1 ▲ Preheat the oven to 160°C/325°F/Gas 3. Season the flour with salt and pepper and spread it out in a shallow bowl. Add the pieces of veal and turn them in the flour until evenly coated. Shake off any excess flour.

2 ▲ Slice one of the onions and separate it into rings. Heat the oil in a large flameproof casserole, then add the veal, with the onion rings, and brown the veal on both sides over a medium heat. Remove the veal shanks with tongs and set aside on kitchen paper to drain.

3 ▲ Chop the remaining onion and add it to the pan with the celery, carrot and garlic. Stir the bottom of the pan to incorporate the pan juices and sediment. Cook gently, stirring frequently, for about 5 minutes until the vegetables soften slightly.

4 ▲ Add the chopped tomatoes, wine, stock, lemon rind and bay leaves, then season to taste with salt and pepper. Bring to the boil, stirring. Return the veal to the pan and coat with the sauce. Cover and cook in the oven for 2 hours or until the veal feels tender when pierced with a fork.

5 Meanwhile, make the gremolata. In a small bowl, mix together the chopped parsley, lemon rind and chopped garlic. Remove the casserole from the oven and lift out and discard the strip of lemon rind and the bay leaves. Taste the sauce for seasoning.

6 Serve the osso buco hot, sprinkled with the gremolata and garnished with extra bay leaves, if you like. Rice, risotto or a simple salad all make excellent accompaniments.

Cook's Tip

Osso buco is available from large supermarkets and good butchers. Choose pieces about 2 cm/¾ in thick.

Beef Stew with Tomatoes, Wine and Peas

Spezzatino

It seems there are as many spezzatino recipes as there are Italian cooks. This one is very traditional, perfect for a hearty and warming winter lunch or dinner. Serve it with boiled or mashed potatoes to soak up the deliciously rich sauce.

Ingredients

30 ml/2 tbsp plain (all-purpose) flour
10 ml/2 tsp chopped fresh thyme
1 kg/2¼ lb braising or stewing steak, cut into large cubes
45 ml/3 tbsp olive oil
1 medium onion, roughly chopped
450 g/1 lb jar sugocasa or passata (bottled strained tomatoes)
250 ml/8 fl oz/1 cup beef stock
250 ml/8 fl oz/1 cup red wine
2 garlic cloves, crushed
30 ml/2 tbsp tomato purée (paste)
275 g/10 oz/2 cups shelled fresh peas
5 ml/1 tsp sugar
salt and freshly ground black pepper
fresh thyme, to garnish

serves 4

1 ▲ Preheat the oven to 160°C/325°F/Gas 3. Put the flour in a shallow dish and season with the thyme and salt and pepper. Add the beef cubes and coat evenly.

2 ▲ Heat the oil in a large flameproof casserole, add the beef and brown on all sides over a medium to high heat. Remove with a slotted spoon and drain on kitchen paper.

3 ▲ Add the onion to the pan, scraping the base of the pan to mix in any sediment. Cook gently for about 3 minutes, stirring frequently, until softened, then stir in the sugocasa or passata, stock, wine, garlic and tomato purée. Bring to the boil, stirring. Return the beef to the pan and stir well to coat with the sauce. Cover and cook in the oven for 1½ hours.

4 ▲ Stir the peas and sugar into the stew. Return the casserole to the oven and cook for 30 minutes more, or until the beef is tender. Taste for seasoning. Garnish with fresh thyme before serving.

Variation

Use thawed frozen peas instead of fresh. Add them 10 minutes before the end of cooking.

Meatballs with Peperonata

Polpette di manzo

These taste very good with creamed potatoes. Use a potato ricer to get them really smooth.

Ingredients

400 g/14 oz minced (ground) beef
115 g/4 oz/2 cups fresh white breadcrumbs
50 g/2 oz/$^{2}/_{3}$ cup grated Parmesan cheese
2 eggs, beaten
pinch of paprika
pinch of grated nutmeg
5 ml/1 tsp dried mixed herbs
2 thin slices of mortadella or prosciutto (total weight about 50 g/2 oz), chopped
vegetable oil, for shallow frying
salt and freshly ground black pepper
chopped fresh basil leaves, to garnish

For the peperonata

30 ml/2 tbsp olive oil
1 small onion, thinly sliced
2 yellow (bell) peppers, cored, seeded and cut lengthways into thin strips
2 red (bell) peppers, cored, seeded and cut lengthways into thin strips
275 g/10 oz/1$^{1}/_{4}$ cups finely chopped tomatoes or passata (bottled strained tomatoes)
15 ml/1 tbsp chopped fresh parsley

serves 4

1 ▲ Put the minced beef in a bowl. Add half the breadcrumbs and all the remaining ingredients, including salt and ground black pepper to taste. Mix well with clean wet hands. Divide the mixture into 12 equal portions and roll each into a ball. Flatten the meat balls slightly so they are about 1 cm/$^{1}/_{2}$ in thick.

2 Put the remaining breadcrumbs on a plate and roll the meatballs in them, a few at a time, until they are evenly coated. Place on a plate, cover with clear film (plastic wrap) and chill for about 30 minutes to firm up.

3 ▲ Meanwhile, make the peperonata. Heat the oil in a medium pan, add the onion and cook gently for about 3 minutes, stirring frequently, until softened. Add the pepper strips and cook for 3 minutes, stirring constantly. Stir in the tomatoes or passata and parsley, with salt and pepper to taste. Bring to the boil, stirring. Cover and cook for about 15 minutes, then remove the lid and continue to cook, stirring frequently, for 10 minutes more, or until reduced and thick. Taste for seasoning. Keep hot.

4 ▲ Pour oil into a frying pan to a depth of about 2.5 cm/1 in. When hot but not smoking, shallow fry the meatballs for 10 - 12 minutes, turning them 3 - 4 times and pressing them flat with a fish slice. Remove and drain on kitchen paper. Serve hot, with the peperonata alongside. Garnish with the basil.

Variation

Instead of minced beef, used half minced pork and half minced veal.

Desserts

An everyday Italian meal usually concludes with fresh fruit. Desserts are reserved for special occasions, and are often bought in from the local pasticceria or gelateria. This is not to say that sweet things are unpopular, but they are usually eaten with a cup of espresso coffee at other times of the day.

Tiramisù

Tiramisù

The name of this popular dessert translates as "pick me up", which is said to derive from the fact that it is so good that it literally makes you swoon when you eat it. There are many, many versions, and the recipe can be adapted to suit your own taste – you can vary the amount of mascarpone, eggs, sponge fingers, coffee and liqueur.

Ingredients

3 eggs, separated
450 g/1 lb/2 cups mascarpone cheese, at room temperature
1 sachet of vanilla sugar
175 ml/6 fl oz/¾ cup cold, very strong, black coffee
120 ml/4 fl oz/½ cup Kahlúa or other coffee-flavoured liqueur
18 savoiardi (Italian sponge fingers)
sifted cocoa powder and grated dark chocolate, to finish

serves 6–8

1 ▲ Put the egg whites in a grease-free bowl and whisk with an electric mixer until stiff and in peaks.

2 ▲ Mix the mascarpone, vanilla sugar and egg yolks in a separate large bowl and whisk with the electric mixer until evenly combined. Fold in the egg whites, then put a few spoonfuls of the mixture in the bottom of a large serving bowl and spread it out evenly.

3 ▲ Mix the coffee and liqueur together in a shallow dish. Dip a sponge finger in the mixture, turn it quickly so that it becomes saturated but does not disintegrate, and place it on top of the mascarpone in the bowl. Add five more dipped sponge fingers, placing them side by side.

4 ▲ Spoon in about one-third of the remaining mixture and spread it out. Make more layers in the same way, ending with mascarpone. Level the surface, then sift cocoa powder all over. Cover and chill overnight. Before serving, sprinkle with cocoa and grated chocolate.

Stuffed Peaches with Amaretto

Pesche ripiene

Together amaretti and amaretto liqueur have an intense almond flavour, and they make a natural companion for peaches, which are plentiful all over Italy.

Ingredients
4 ripe but firm peaches
50 g/2 oz amaretti
25 g/1 oz/2 tbsp butter, softened
25 g/1 oz/2 tbsp caster (superfine) sugar
1 egg yolk
60 ml/4 tbsp amaretto liqueur
250 ml/8 fl oz/1 cup dry white wine
8 tiny sprigs of basil, to decorate
ice cream or pouring cream (half-and-half), to serve
serves 4

1 ▲ Preheat the oven to 180°C/350°F/ Gas 4. Following the natural indentation line on each peach, cut in half down to the central stone (pit), then twist the halves in opposite directions to separate them. Remove the peach stones, then cut away a little of the central flesh to make a larger hole for the stuffing. Chop this flesh finely and set aside.

2 ▲ Put the amaretti in a bowl and crush them finely with the end of a rolling pin.

3 ▲ Cream the butter and sugar together in a separate bowl until smooth. Stir in the reserved chopped peach flesh, the egg yolk and half the amaretto liqueur with the amaretti crumbs. Lightly butter a baking dish that is just large enough to hold the peach halves in a single layer.

4 ▲ Spoon the stuffing into the peaches, then stand them in the dish. Mix the remaining liqueur with the wine, pour over the peaches and bake for 25 minutes or until the peaches feel tender when tested with a skewer. Decorate with basil and serve at once, with ice cream or cream.

Zabaglione

Zabaglione

This sumptuous warm dessert is very quick and easy to make, but it does need to be served straight away. For a dinner party, assemble all the ingredients and equipment ahead of time so that all you have to do is quickly mix everything together once the main course is over.

Ingredients
4 egg yolks
65 g/2 1/2 oz/1/3 cup caster (superfine) sugar
120 ml/4 fl oz/1/2 cup dry Marsala
savoiardi (Italian sponge fingers), to serve
serves 6

Cook's Tip
When whisking the egg yolks, make sure that the bottom of the bowl does not touch the water or the egg yolks will scramble.

1 ▲ Half fill a pan with water and bring it to simmering point. Put the egg yolks and sugar in a large heatproof bowl and beat with a hand-held electric mixer until pale and creamy.

2 ▲ Put the bowl over the pan and gradually pour in the Marsala, whisking the mixture until it is very thick and has increased in volume.

3 Remove the bowl from the water and pour the zabaglione into six heatproof, long-stemmed glasses. Serve at once, with sponge fingers.

Lovers' Knots

Cenci

The literal translation of cenci is "rags and tatters", but they are often referred to by the more endearing term of lovers' knots. They are eaten at carnival time in February.

Ingredients
150 g/5 oz/1 1/4 cups plain (all-purpose) flour
2.5 ml/1/2 tsp baking powder
pinch of salt
30 ml/2 tbsp caster (superfine) sugar, plus extra for dusting
1 egg, beaten
about 25 ml/1 1/2 tbsp rum
vegetable oil, for deep frying
makes 24

Cook's Tip
If you do not have a deep-fat fryer with a built-in thermostat, or a deep-fat thermometer, test the temperature of the oil before deep frying by dropping in a scrap of the dough trimmings – it should turn crisp and golden in about 30 seconds.

1 ▲ Sift the flour, baking powder and salt into a bowl, then stir in the sugar. Add the egg. Stir with a fork until it is evenly mixed with the flour, then add the rum gradually and continue mixing until the dough draws together. Knead the dough on a lightly floured surface until it is smooth. Divide the dough into quarters.

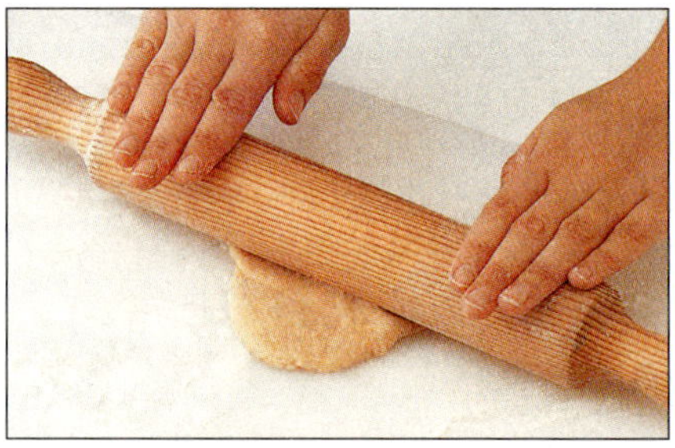

2 ▲ Roll each piece out to a 15 x 7.5 cm/ 6 x 3 in rectangle and trim to make them straight. Cut each rectangle lengthways into six strips, 1 cm/ 1/2 in wide, and tie into a simple knot.

3 Heat the oil in a deep-fat fryer to a temperature of 190°C/375°F. Deep fry the knots in batches for 1–2 minutes until crisp and golden. Transfer to kitchen paper with a slotted spoon. Serve warm, dusted with sugar.

Fresh Orange Granita

Granita all'arancia

A granita is like a water ice, but coarser and quite grainy in texture, hence its name. It makes a refreshing dessert after a rich main course, or a cooling treat on a hot summer's day.

Ingredients

4 large oranges
1 large lemon
150 g/5 oz/ ³/₄ cup sugar
475 ml/16 fl oz/2 cups water
blanched pared strips of orange and lemon rind, to decorate
dessert biscuits (cookies), to serve
serves 6

1 ▲ Thinly pare the rind from the oranges and lemon, taking care to avoid the bitter white pith, and set aside for the decoration. Cut the fruit in half and squeeze the juice into a jug. Set aside.

2 Heat the sugar and water in a heavy-based pan, stirring over a gentle heat until the sugar dissolves. Bring to the boil, then boil without stirring for about 10 minutes, until a syrup forms.

3 ▲ Remove the syrup from the heat, add the pieces of orange and lemon rind and shake the pan. Cover and allow to cool.

4 ▲ Strain the sugar syrup into a shallow freezer container and add the fruit juice. Stir well to mix, then freeze, uncovered, for about 4 hours until slushy.

Cook's Tip

To make the decoration, slice extra orange and lemon rind into thin strips. Blanch for 2 minutes, refresh under cold water and dry before use.

5 ▲ Remove the half-frozen mixture from the freezer and mix with a fork, then return to the freezer and freeze again for 4 hours more or until frozen hard. To serve, turn into a bowl and allow to soften for about 10 minutes, then break up with a fork again and pile into long-stemmed glasses. Decorate with the strips of orange and lemon rind and serve with dessert biscuits.

Apple Cake

Torta di mele

This moist cake is best served warm. It comes from Genoa, home of the whisked sponge. When whipping the cream, add grated lemon rind – it tastes delicious.

Ingredients
675 g/1½ lb eating apples
finely grated rind and juice of 1 lemon
4 eggs
150 g/5 oz/¾ cup caster (superfine) sugar
150 g/5 oz/1¼ cups plain (all-purpose) flour
5 ml/1 tsp baking powder
pinch of salt
115 g/4 oz/½ cup butter, melted and cooled, plus extra for greasing
1 sachet of vanilla sugar, for sprinkling
very finely pared strips of citrus rind, to decorate
whipped cream, to serve
serves 6

1 ▲ Preheat the oven to 180°C/350°F/ Gas 4. Brush a 23 cm/9 in springform tin (pan) with melted butter and line the base with baking parchment. Quarter, core and peel the apples, then slice thinly. Put the slices in a bowl and pour over the lemon juice.

2 ▲ Put the eggs, sugar and lemon rind in a bowl and whisk with a hand-held electric mixer until the mixture is thick and mousse-like. The whisks should leave a trail.

3 ▲ Sift half the flour, all the baking powder and the salt over the egg mousse, then fold in gently with a large metal spoon. Slowly drizzle in the melted butter from the side of the bowl and fold it in gently with the spoon. Sift over the remaining flour, fold it in gently, then add the apples and fold these in equally gently.

4 ▲ Spoon into the prepared tin and level the surface. Bake for 40 minutes or until a skewer comes out clean. Leave to settle in the tin for about 10 minutes, then invert on a wire rack. Turn the cake the right way up and sprinkle the vanilla sugar over the top. Decorate with the citrus rind. Serve warm, with whipped cream.

Sicilian Ricotta Cake

Cassata siciliana

The word cassata is often used to describe a layered ice cream cake. In Sicily, however, it is a traditional cake made of layers of sponge, ricotta cheese and candied peel, infused with alcohol, and it looks and tastes truly delicious.

Ingredients
675 g/1½ lb/3 cups ricotta cheese
finely grated rind of 1 orange
2 sachets of vanilla sugar
75 ml/5 tbsp orange-flavoured liqueur
115 g/4 oz candied peel
8 trifle sponge cakes
60 ml/4 tbsp freshly squeezed orange juice
extra candied peel, to decorate
serves 8–10

1 ▲ Push the ricotta cheese through a sieve (strainer) into a bowl, add the orange rind, vanilla sugar and 15 ml/1 tbsp of the liqueur and beat well to mix. Transfer about one-third of the mixture to another bowl, cover and chill until serving time.

2 ▲ Finely chop the candied peel and beat into the remaining ricotta cheese mixture until evenly mixed. Set aside while you prepare the tin (pan).

3 ▲ Line the base of a 1.2 litre/2 pint/5 cup loaf tin with baking parchment. Cut the trifle sponges in half through their thickness. Arrange four pieces of sponge side by side in the bottom of the loaf tin and sprinkle with 15 ml/1 tbsp each of liqueur and orange juice.

4 ▲ Put one-third of the ricotta and fruit mixture in the tin and spread it out evenly. Cover with four more pieces of sponge and sprinkle with another 15 ml/1 tbsp each liqueur and orange juice as before.

5 Repeat the alternate layers of ricotta mixture and sponge until all the ingredients are used, soaking the sponge pieces with liqueur and orange juice each time, and ending with soaked sponge. Cover with a piece of baking parchment.

6 ▲ Cut a piece of card to fit inside the tin, place on top of the baking parchment and weight down evenly. Chill for 24 hours.

7 To serve, remove the weights, card and paper and run a palette knife between the sides of the cassata and the tin. Invert a serving plate on top of the cassata, then carefully invert the two so that the cassata is upside down on the plate. Peel off the lining paper.

8 Spread the chilled ricotta mixture over the cassata to cover it completely, then decorate the top with candied peel, cut into fancy shapes. Serve chilled.

Cook's Tip
Don't worry if the cassata has pressed into an uneven shape when turned out. This will be disguised when the cake is covered in the chilled ricotta mixture.

Ricotta Pudding

Budino di ricotta

This creamy, rich dessert is very easy to make and, as it can be made up to 24 hours ahead, it is ideal for a dinner party. The combination of ricotta cheese and candied fruits is very popular in Sicily, where this recipe originated.

Ingredients
225 g/8 oz/1 cup ricotta cheese
50 g/2 oz/⅓ cup candied fruits
60 ml/4 tbsp sweet Marsala
250 ml/8 fl oz/1 cup double (heavy) cream
50 g/2 oz/¼ cup caster (superfine) sugar, plus extra to serve
finely grated rind of 1 orange
350 g/12 oz/2 cups fresh raspberries
strips of thinly pared orange rind, to decorate
serves 4–6

Cook's Tip
Buy candied fruits in large pieces from a good delicatessen – tubs of chopped candied peel are too tough to eat raw, and should only be used in baking.

1 ▲ Press the ricotta through a sieve (strainer) into a bowl. Finely chop the candied fruits and stir into the sieved (strained) ricotta with half of the Marsala. Put the cream, sugar and orange rind in another bowl and whip together until the cream is standing in soft peaks.

2 ▲ Fold the whipped cream into the ricotta mixture. Spoon into individual glass serving bowls and top with the raspberries. Chill until serving time. Sprinkle with the remaining Marsala and dust the top of each bowl liberally with caster sugar just before serving. Decorate with the orange rind.

Coffee and Chocolate Bombe

Zuccotto

In Italy the commercial ice cream is so good that no one would dream of making their own ice cream for this dessert. Assembling the zuccotto is impressive enough in itself.

Ingredients

15–18 savoiardi (Italian sponge fingers)
about 175 ml/6 fl oz/¾ cup sweet Marsala
75 g/3 oz amaretti
about 475 ml/16 fl oz/2 cups coffee ice cream, softened
about 475 ml/16 fl oz/2 cups vanilla ice cream, softened
50 g/2 oz dark chocolate, grated
chocolate curls and sifted cocoa powder or icing (confectioners') sugar, to decorate

serves 6–8

1 ▲ Line a 1 litre/1¾ pint/4 cup bowl with a large piece of damp muslin (cheesecloth), letting it hang over the top edge. Trim the sponge fingers to fit the basin. Pour the Marsala into a shallow dish. Dip a sponge finger in the Marsala, turning it quickly so that it becomes saturated but does not disintegrate. Stand it against the side of the bowl, sugared-side out. Repeat with the remaining sponge fingers to line the bowl fully.

2 Fill in the base and any gaps around the side with any trimmings and savoiardi cut to fit. Chill for about 30 minutes.

Cook's Tip

In Italy there are special dome-shaped moulds for making this dessert, the name for which comes from the Italian word zucca, meaning pumpkin. The shape will not be quite the same when it is made in an ordinary bowl but the result will still look impressive and taste delicious.

3 ▲ Put the amaretti in a large bowl and crush them with a rolling pin. Add the coffee ice cream and any remaining Marsala and beat until mixed. Spoon into the sponge-finger-lined bowl.

4 Press the ice cream against the sponge to form an even layer with a hollow. Freeze for 2 hours.

5 Put the vanilla ice cream and grated chocolate in a bowl and beat together until evenly mixed. Spoon into the hollow in the centre of the mould. Smooth the top, then cover with the overhanging muslin. Place in the freezer overnight.

6 To serve, run a metal spatula between the muslin and the basin, then unfold the top of the muslin. Invert a chilled serving plate on top of the zuccotto, then invert the two so that the zuccotto is upside down on the plate. Carefully peel off the muslin. Decorate the zuccotto with the chocolate curls, then sift cocoa powder or icing sugar over. Serve at once.

Index